Current
CONTROVERSIES

Politics and Religion

Other Books in the Current Controversies Series

Politics and Religion

Debra A. Miller, Book Editor

GREENHAVEN PRESS
A part of Gale, Cengage Learning

Detroit • New York • San Francisco • New Haven, Conn • Waterville, Maine • London

Elizabeth Des Chenes, *Director, Publishing Solutions*

© 2013 Greenhaven Press, a part of Gale, Cengage Learning

Gale and Greenhaven Press are registered trademarks used herein under license.

For more information, contact:
Greenhaven Press
27500 Drake Rd.
Farmington Hills, MI 48331-3535
Or you can visit our Internet site at gale.cengage.com

For product information and technology assistance, contact us at

Gale Customer Support, 1-800-877-4253
For permission to use material from this text or product, submit all requests online at www.cengage.com/permissions

Further permissions questions can be emailed to permissionrequest@cengage.com

Articles in Greenhaven Press anthologies are often edited for length to meet page requirements. In addition, original titles of these works are changed to clearly present the main thesis and to explicitly indicate the author's opinion. Every effort is made to ensure that Greenhaven Press accurately reflects the original intent of the authors. Every effort has been made to trace the owners of copyrighted material.

Cover image © Frederick Bass/fStop/Alamy.

LIBRARY OF CONGRESS CATALOGING-IN-PUBLICATION DATA

Politics and religion / Debra A. Miller, book editor.
    pages cm. -- (Current controversies)
    Includes bibliographical references and index.
    ISBN 978-0-7377-6884-8 -- ISBN 978-0-7377-6885-5 (pbk.)
    1. Religion and politics. I. Miller, Debra A., editor of compilation.
    BL65.P7P6377 2013
    322'.1--dc23
                                     2012051657

Printed in the United States of America
1 2 3 4 5   17 16 15 14 13

Contents

Christian evangelicals have changed conservatism into a religious movement over the last several decades. The United States used to have a liberal democracy that featured negotiation with respect for minority views, but the new religion-based conservatism asserts beliefs that cannot be compromised and are not susceptible to logical arguments.

Chapter 2: Does Government Interfere with Religious Freedom?

The Barack Obama administration's action to require religious employers to provide health insurance coverage for government-approved contraceptive methods, sterilization procedures, and related education and counseling is a serious erosion of religious freedoms, especially for Catholics who oppose contraception and their religiously affiliated medical institutions. The government should exempt religious institutions from this requirement.

Chapter 3: What Role Does Religion Play in International Politics?

Election of Islamic political parties in Middle East nations such as Morocco, Tunisia, and Egypt following political uprisings there indicate that the Arab Spring has led to a rise of political Islam. Egypt will be a good test case for what role Islam will play in government and whether a fundamentalist or liberal form of Islam will prevail.

US policymakers have historically associated secular government with democracy and good government and Islamist governments with bad governance. However, this view often empowered dictators, and after the political uprising in Egypt that overthrew an autocratic government, it is time to give real democracy a chance in Muslim-majority countries.

Chapter 4: How Should the United States Balance Religion and Politics in the Future?

Rodney K. Smith

President Barack Obama violated Roman Catholics' religious liberty by mandating that religious institutions provide insurance coverage for contraceptives, continuing a US trend toward undermining religious freedoms. The president can redeem himself by supporting a constitutional amendment requiring a compelling state interest before government acts to regulate religion.

Oliver Thomas

Historically, US law used a balancing test to determine how much the government could restrict religious freedom, but some states are proposing more radical measures to limit government actions. These ideas would move the nation toward a theocracy—a step too far.

Armando Lloréns-Sar

The Obama administration has failed to defend the idea of separation of church and state—a principle that both ensures freedom of religion and protects the government from being overtaken by religion. Religious institutions that own public accommodations should not be exempted from secular laws.

Foreword

By definition, controversies are "discussions of questions in which opposing opinions clash" (*Webster's Twentieth Century Dictionary Unabridged*). Few would deny that controversies are a pervasive part of the human condition and exist on virtually every level of human enterprise. Controversies transpire between individuals and among groups, within nations and between nations. Controversies supply the grist necessary for progress by providing challenges and challengers to the status quo. They also create atmospheres where strife and warfare can flourish. A world without controversies would be a peaceful world; but it also would be, by and large, static and prosaic.

The Series' Purpose

The purpose of the Current Controversies series is to explore many of the social, political, and economic controversies dominating the national and international scenes today. Titles selected for inclusion in the series are highly focused and specific. For example, from the larger category of criminal justice, Current Controversies deals with specific topics such as police brutality, gun control, white collar crime, and others. The debates in Current Controversies also are presented in a useful, timeless fashion. Articles and book excerpts included in each title are selected if they contribute valuable, long-range ideas to the overall debate. And wherever possible, current information is enhanced with historical documents and other relevant materials. Thus, while individual titles are current in focus, every effort is made to ensure that they will not become quickly outdated. Books in the Current Controversies series will remain important resources for librarians, teachers, and students for many years.

In addition to keeping the titles focused and specific, great care is taken in the editorial format of each book in the series. Book introductions and chapter prefaces are offered to provide background material for readers. Chapters are organized around several key questions that are answered with diverse opinions representing all points on the political spectrum. Materials in each chapter include opinions in which authors clearly disagree as well as alternative opinions in which authors may agree on a broader issue but disagree on the possible solutions. In this way, the content of each volume in Current Controversies mirrors the mosaic of opinions encountered in society. Readers will quickly realize that there are many viable answers to these complex issues. By questioning each author's conclusions, students and casual readers can begin to develop the critical thinking skills so important to evaluating opinionated material.

Current Controversies is also ideal for controlled research. Each anthology in the series is composed of primary sources taken from a wide gamut of informational categories including periodicals, newspapers, books, US and foreign government documents, and the publications of private and public organizations. Readers will find factual support for reports, debates, and research papers covering all areas of important issues. In addition, an annotated table of contents, an index, a book and periodical bibliography, and a list of organizations to contact are included in each book to expedite further research.

Perhaps more than ever before in history, people are confronted with diverse and contradictory information. During the Persian Gulf War, for example, the public was not only treated to minute-to-minute coverage of the war, it was also inundated with critiques of the coverage and countless analyses of the factors motivating US involvement. Being able to sort through the plethora of opinions accompanying today's major issues, and to draw one's own conclusions, can be a complicated and frustrating struggle. It is the editors' hope that Current Controversies will help readers with this struggle.

Introduction

"Although the phrase 'separation of church and state' does not appear in the US Constitution, it is widely used and accepted as a constitutional principle."

The United States is known around the world as a secular democracy that embraces the principle of separation of church and state. Unlike the constitutions of many other countries, the US Constitution makes no references to a deity or to a specific religion. Instead, the First Amendment to the Constitution contains the establishment clause, which states that "Congress shall make no law respecting an establishment of religion, or prohibiting the free exercise thereof." This clause simultaneously guarantees both separation of religion from government and the freedom citizens have regarding their religious practice. Yet some US public buildings are decorated with references to God; US currency includes the statement, "In God We Trust"; and US presidents and members of Congress are sworn in by placing their right hand on the Bible or another religious text of their choosing, such as the Koran. The separation of church and state persists, despite the fact that, historically, the majority of Americans have been Christian, and many interpret the work of the Founding Fathers as based on Christian values. In the early 2000s, many US Christians are pushing to expand the role of religion in US policies, politics, and public life, while others assert that government is secular and restrained by law from acting on or affecting religions and religious practice.

The unity of church and state existed in Europe for centuries; governments of many countries were linked with or functioned as one with a national church—an arrangement that prompted religious intolerance and fueled religious wars.

Henry VIII in England, for example, established himself in the early 1500s as the head of the Church of England (also called the Anglican Church), and in reaction to the controlling dictates of the Anglican Church nonconformist minority groups of protestants, among them Puritans, ultimately sought religious freedom by emigrating to North America. These individuals espoused the importance of religious freedom as a separate right over which government ought not to have any power. In the early 1600s, such protesting groups settled many places in modern-day Massachusetts. These included Congregationalists, Calvinistic Presbyterians, Quakers, and other independent sects, and it was members of these diverse Christian but mostly non-Catholic sects who established the thirteen original North American colonies.

Despite their affirmation of freedom of religion, however, many early colonists were intolerant toward other religions. The Puritans, for example, wanted to practice their own religion freely but did not approve of others doing the same, whom they called heathens. In colonial Massachusetts, Puritan zealotry led to the infamous Salem witch trials in 1692 and 1693, in which over fifty people were charged with witchcraft and nearly nineteen were executed. In Virginia, one of the most populated colonies, even the oppressive Church of England found a foothold, sending Anglican missionaries and clergy, who collected taxes from parishioners to run local governments and pay for roads and relief for the poor. In fact, nine of the original thirteen colonies established a state religion, giving churches a great deal of power over political affairs in colonial North America.

By the time of the American Revolution (1775–1783) and the writing of the US Constitution (signed in 1787), many were concerned about the role religion would play in the new nation. Shapers of the Constitution wanted to avoid the religious turmoil and wars that had afflicted European countries for so many centuries. Thomas Jefferson, in particular, felt strongly that there should be no established state religion in the new nation, and he began an effort to guarantee freedom *of* religion as well as freedom *from* religion in his home state of Virginia. In 1777, Jefferson drafted a law—An Act for Establishing Religious Freedom—which was introduced into the Virginia legislature once he became governor in 1779. Although Jefferson's bill was opposed by the Anglican Church, it drew support from other religious groups such as the Baptists, Presbyterians, and Jews who wanted protection from religious persecution. With the help of James Madison, the religious freedom bill passed in the state legislature in 1786, the year before the US Constitution was adopted by the Constitutional Convention in Philadelphia in 1787.

In 1789, the founding fathers, including Jefferson, wrote the first ten amendments to the new Constitution, which came to be known as the Bill of Rights. The First Amendment contained the freedom of religion and establishment of religion clause: "Congress shall make no law respecting an establishment of religion, or prohibiting the free exercise thereof. . . ." Jefferson's Virginia law served as a model for this constitutional protection. The Bill of Rights was adopted by the House of Representatives on August 21, 1789, and went into effect on December 15, 1791, after a process of ratification by three-fourths of the states. Much later, the Fourteenth Amendment was added to the US Constitution, making all the protections of the First Amendment applicable at the state level. As a result, neither the federal government nor the states' governments can establish a national or state religion, and freedom of religion is a right guaranteed for all Americans.

Jefferson was proud of his role in bringing freedom of religion to Virginia and the nation. In 1802, when he was president of the United States, Jefferson wrote a letter to the Danbury Baptist Association of Connecticut, explaining the meaning of the First Amendment's clause prohibiting a government establishment of religion. This letter contains the first known reference to the often repeated phrase "separation of church and state." Jefferson's letter stated, in part:

> I contemplate with solemn reverence that act of the whole American people which declared that their legislature should make no law respecting an establishment of religion, or prohibiting the free exercise thereof, thus building a wall of separation between church and state. . . .[1]

James Madison, too, wrote about the need for separation between religion and government. The US Supreme Court subsequently interpreted the First Amendment to require a wall of separation between church and state, just as Jefferson and Madison said, so that government is prohibited from adopting any particular religion as an official religion, and it must avoid excessive involvement in religion.

Although the phrase "separation of church and state" does not appear in the US Constitution, it is widely used and accepted as a constitutional principle. Nevertheless, the degree to which religion should be separated from government continues to be debated. The authors of the viewpoints in *Current Controversies: Politics and Religion* offer different views about issues such as whether religion should play a role in US politics, whether government is interfering too much with freedom of religion, whether religion is having an undue influence on international politics, and how the United States should balance religion and politics in the future.

Notes

1. Select works of Thomas Jefferson, Constitutional Society, www.constitution.org/tj/sep_church_state.htm.

CHAPTER 1

Should Religion Play a Role in US Politics?

Chapter Preface

Since the 1970s, conservative Christian political groups, including Christian Evangelicals, conservative Catholics, and Mormons, have influenced US politics. Christian conservatives, often simply called Evangelicals because of the large numbers of Evangelical/fundamentalist Christians involved, have historically supported socially conservative policies that they believe exemplify their religious and family values. Key issues for these groups include opposition to abortion and opposition to same-sex marriage, but many Christian conservatives have tended to support conservative fiscal and foreign policy positions as well. In the early 2000s, the Tea Party emerged, a conservative, loosely organized coalition of political groups named partly after the 1773 Boston Tea Party and partly for the "TEA" acronym that signifies the phrase: "taxed enough already." The Tea Party followers generally believe that the federal government has grown too powerful and too fiscally irresponsible, and they push for smaller government, lower taxes, reduced federal debt, and a balanced federal budget. According to a 2012 analysis by author David Brody, the Tea Party has combined with the Evangelical movement to create a new political force that he calls the "Teavangelicals." Brody explains his theory in his book, *The Teavangelicals: The Inside Story of How the Evangelicals and the Tea Party Are Taking Back America*.

The Teavangelical movement, according to Brody, began with the founding of the Moral Majority, a Christian right political organization formed by Reverend Jerry Falwell (1933–2007) in 1979. Falwell was the pastor of the huge Thomas Road Baptist Church in Lynchburg, Virginia. He also was a televangelist who preached on a television program, *Old Time Gospel Hour*. In 1976, Falwell decided to abandon the traditional Baptist position on separating religion and politics and scheduled a series of "I Love America" tours across the United States to raise support for the creation of a national religion-based political organization. The tours proved successful, and Falwell in 1979 created the Moral Majority group to unite and rally religious conservatives to lobby for conservative political causes. Commentators have characterized the Moral Majority as a reaction to what conservatives view as the moral decay of the 1960s—sexual permissiveness, feminism, gay rights, and secularism.

During his time on the national and world stage, Falwell became a prominent political commentator on social issues such as abortion and gay rights. He and his group opposed *Roe v. Wade*, the 1973 Supreme Court case that legalized abortion, and fought against expanding civil rights of gays and lesbians. In 1980, many commentators credited the Moral Majority with helping to elect Republican presidential candidate Ronald Reagan as well as many conservative congressmen. Although the Moral Majority was disbanded about a decade after it began, the influence of the Christian right continued. The Christian Coalition, a political group founded by Pat Robertson, another charismatic televangelist preacher, successfully infiltrated the ranks of the Republican Party, culminating in the 2000 presidential election (and 2004 reelection) of George W. Bush, who reportedly was born again as an evangelical Christian in 1985.

On the one hand, many commentators argue that the Christian right's political influence waned during the Bush administration. Although President Bush established the Office of Faith-Based Initiatives, designed to help faith-based social and charity organizations win millions in federal funding, the Christian right was unable to convince Congress to pass conservative-backed laws that would have allowed state and local governments to become more entwined with religion and permitted churches to directly fund political campaigns. On the other hand, commentators have noted that the religious right was successful in getting President Bush to ban US foreign aid for any family planning organization abroad that either performed legal abortions or provided information about abortion, and in limiting the availability of abortion in US states. Religious lobbyists also continue to push on other political issues, such as allowing creationism to be taught with evolution in school science classes, opposing same-sex marriage, and changing the US Constitution to alter the separation of church and state.

One incarnation of the religious right appears to be within the Tea Party, which began in 2009 largely as a nonreligious protest movement with libertarian political views modeled on those of perennial presidential candidate Ron Paul. Like Ron Paul, early Tea Party protesters generally complained that the federal government has grown too big, that it taxes citizens too much, and that it has taken on too much debt. The Tea Party endorsed a number of candidates to run in the Republican primaries in preparation for the 2010 midterm congressional and state elections, and many of those candidates won, ousting longterm, mainstream Republican incumbents. Between 2009 and 2012, many commentators concluded that the Tea Party had pushed Republican congressional members to become increasingly conservative, especially on fiscal and deficit issues, and had stymied the efforts of Democratic president Barack Obama to find compromises on a range of important matters. In addition, the Tea Party seems to have attracted a wider following made up largely of members of the religious right. According to author David Brody, 50 to 60 percent of Tea Party supporters as of 2012 were conservative Christians. Tea Party fiscal conservatives with evangelical Christians who care deeply about conservative social issues were intent on being a factor in the 2012 presidential and congressional elections, as well as in the future. The authors of the viewpoints included in this chapter debate the central question of what role religion should play in US politics.

Religion and Politics Are Inseparable

Pierre Whalon

Pierre Whalon is the bishop in charge of the Convocation of Episcopal Churches in Europe, based in Paris, France. He is also a columnist and feature writer for both secular and religious publications and blogs.

Cardinal Timothy Dolan appeared on *Face the Nation* on Easter Sunday [2012]. The *New York Times* reported on the conversation.

Asked by . . . [TV moderator Bob] Schieffer if he thought religion was playing too much of a role in politics, the cardinal said, "No, I don't think so at all."

"The public square in the United States is always enriched whenever people approach it when they're inspired by their deepest held convictions," he said. "And, on the other hand, Bob, I think the public square is impoverished when people might be coerced to put a piece of duct tape over their mouth, keeping them from bring[ing] their deepest-held convictions to the conversations."

The cardinal of New York also quashed the idea that one should not vote for [presidential candidate] Mitt Romney just because he is a Mormon.

I agree with him on these two points. I can hear, however, the many people who have walked up to me and told me to keep my preacherly nose out of politics: Nevertheless, it should be clear from human history that religion and politics cannot be separated. Both of them arise from the fact that we *Homo sapiens* are communal beings: we cannot live completely alone.

Pierre Whalon, "Religion and Politics Are Inseparable: Get Over It," *The Huffington Post*, April 9, 2012. Copyright © 2012 by Bishop Pierre Whalon. All rights reserved. Reproduced by permission.

Every aspect of what makes us human develops completely from living in a community, beginning with the family. Anthropologists are clear that having a sense of the sacred (whatever one makes of it) is one of the fundamental aspects of what differentiates *Sapiens* from other hominids. Politics is how we order our common life.

Can we reasonably expect people not to bring their deepest convictions, which are always religious in nature, to the public square?

It is therefore impossible to separate them, and anyone who claims it can and should be done is either lying or hasn't thought it through. It's pretty basic. . . .

Religion and Politics Intertwined

There are a lot of national elections happening this year around the world. Name one where religion is not a significant factor, even if it is not blaringly obvious, as it is in the United States. France, for instance, will elect a new president next month, and it is clear that Nicolas Sarkozy has been enlisting the help of religious leaders, including Muslims as well as Catholics and Protestants, in his re-election campaign. Just as obviously, his main rival, Socialist François Hollande, has been complaining about Sarkozy's alleged infringements on the *République laïque*, the legally secular, rigorously neutral French Republic. Atheists are religious too.

As a religious leader, I have often been told, as I said, to "stay out of politics." But that is impossible for a Christian, since Jesus of Nazareth's execution—a crucial moment in human history for us—was blatantly political. Proclaiming his Gospel therefore has inevitable political consequences. When Christians began reciting *Kyrie eleison* ("Lord, have mercy") in the liturgy, it was a powerful political statement. That is what a loyal Roman said to Caesar when coming into the emperor's presence. To repeat that in worship clearly states that God, not the emperor or other political ruler, is in charge. Can't get more political than that, especially considering that Caesar was thought to be divine himself.

Along the same lines, examine the places where religion and politics intersect in other faiths. Here, for example, is the right place to question the beliefs of the Mormons if one of them might become the President of the United States. John Kennedy had to answer similar questions, and his Catholicism was not held against him (just as Romney's religion should not stereotype him). The attempts by some Roman Catholic prelates to use excommunication against politicians who support abortion rights raise similar questions, however. Where does faith end and political loyalty begin? Can we reasonably expect people not to bring their deepest convictions, which are always religious in nature, to the public square, as Cardinal Dolan said?

Separation of Church and State

The separation of church and state is certainly a major advance in human history and political theory. Under no circumstances should religious leaders ever be given political power merely because they are part of a religious hierarchy. Iran provides the latest example of how theocracy always corrupts both religion and politics. That said, all of us, even us bishops, have a duty and a right as citizens to engage in politics, at least by casting a vote. In particular, bishops having sworn to guard the faith and unity of the church must speak out from time to time. As Archbishop Rowan Williams has argued, this still has to be done while respecting the relationship between religion and human rights.

This is where I worry about the way in which the Catholic hierarchy, or the Mormon hierarchy for that matter, may try to influence politics. Dolan's call to his fellow bishops to man the barricades on the health care issue does not seem to me to respect the necessary requirement of all religious leaders' sallies into politics. The only way we bishops (or rabbis, or imams, or prophets, etc.) should publicly intervene in the politics of a democratic society is through linking our particular concern to the common good, not the rights of our particular religion. Nor can we argue purely from revelation: why should other citizens respect our opinions if we do not present them as applicable to all people regardless of religion?

As bishop of a multinational jurisdiction in which there is always some election happening, I always call upon the faithful to go and vote. It is biblical that Christians should care about the society we live in (Romans 13:1–7), and in a democracy, voting is a duty. (I also say that if you don't vote, you have no right to complain.) It would be a perversion of my authority to insist that they vote [for] or against particular candidates, though commenting on political ideologies that in my view threaten the common good is not inappropriate. In other words, it's not so much a matter of "do not vote for candidate X" as it is do not support fascism, racism, etc.

There is always a delicate balance to strike. So much is at stake, for all of us. But let us not kid ourselves, at least: religion and politics are inseparable.

Religious Traditions Can Play a Healthy Role in Politics

Robert Jensen

Robert Jensen is an author, a journalism professor at the University of Texas at Austin, and a board member of the Third Coast Activist Resource Center, a community center in Austin, Texas.

Does God take sides in the elections? Is there a voters' guide hiding in our holy books? Should we pray for electoral inspiration?

Secular people tend to answer an emphatic "NO" to those questions, as do most progressive religious folk. Because religious fundamentalists so often present an easy-to-caricature version of faith-based politics—even to the point of implying that God would want us to vote for certain candidates—it is tempting to want to banish all talk of the divine from political life.

But a blanket claim that "religion and politics don't mix" misunderstands the inevitable connection between the two. Whether secular or religious, our political judgments are always rooted in first principles—claims about what it means to be human that can't be reduced to evidence and logic. Should people act purely out of self-interest, or is solidarity with others just as important? Do we owe loyalty to a nation-state? Under what conditions, if any, is the taking of a human life justified? What is the appropriate relationship of human beings to the larger living world?

These basic moral/spiritual questions underlie everyone's politics, and our answers are shaped by the philosophical and/or theological systems in which we find inspiration and insight. Since everyone's political positions reflect their foundational commitments, it doesn't seem fair to say that those grounded in a secular philosophy can draw on their traditions, but people whose political outlooks are rooted in religion have to mute themselves.

The Tradition of Prophecy

Rather than trying to bracket religion out of politics, we should be discussing how religious traditions can play a role in a healthy politics, and one productive place to start in the context of the Christian tradition is [theologian] Walter Brueggemann's new book, *The Practice of Prophetic Imagination: Preaching an Emancipatory Word*. Building on the book for which he is most known—*The Prophetic Imagination*, first published in 1978 with a second edition in 2001—Brueggemann moves beyond sectarian politics and self-satisfied religion to ask difficult questions about our relationship to power. He makes it clear that taking the prophetic tradition seriously means being willing to make those around us—and ourselves—uncomfortable.

In that earlier book, Brueggemann argued that the tradition of prophecy demands more of us than a self-indulgent expression of righteous indignation over injustice or vague calls for social justice, what he calls "a liberal understanding of prophecy" that can serve as "an attractive and face-saving device for any excessive abrasiveness in the service of almost any cause."

Brueggemann wants more from those who claim to stand in the prophetic tradition, which he asserts is rooted in resistance to the dominance of a "royal consciousness" that produces numbness in people. Prophetic ministry, Brueggemann argues in that first book, seeks to "penetrate the numbness in order to face the body of death in which we are caught" and "penetrate despair so that new futures can be believed in and embraced by us." And make no mistake, Brueggemann's concern is not the royal culture of Biblical days but the dominant culture of the contemporary United States and its quest for endless material acquisition and constant expansion of power.

Brueggemann also makes it clear that the prophet is not a finger-wagging scold. The task of prophetic ministry is to bring to public expression "the dread of endings, the collapse of our self-madness, the barriers and pecking orders that secure us at each other's expense, and the fearful practice of eating off the table of a hungry brother or sister." In other words, prophets speak the language of mourning, "that crying in pathos," that provides "the ultimate form of criticism, for it announces the sure end of the whole royal arrangement."

More than three decades after the publication of that book, Brueggemann returns to explore the implications of taking seriously the prophetic imagination, specifically for clergy. But while the book is aimed at preachers and their struggles to bring the prophetic imagination alive in a congregation, Brueggemann's words are relevant to any citizen concerned about the health of our politics and the state of the world.

Contemporary preachers need to connect the dots and make a case that goes against the grain.

The new book begins by arguing that the gospel narrative of social transformation, justice, and compassion is in direct conflict with the dominant narrative of the United States: "therapeutic, technological, consumerist militarism" that "is committed to the notion of self-invention in the pursuit of self-sufficiency." The logic and goals of that dominant culture foster "competitive productivity, motivated by pervasive anxiety about having enough, or being enough, or being in control." All this bolsters notions of "US exceptionalism that gives warrant to the usurpations pursuit of commodities in the name of freedom, at the expense of the neighbor."

Right out of the gate, Brueggemann makes it clear that he is going to critique not just the problems of the moment but the political, economic, and social systems from which those problems emerge, and that to speak frankly about those systems means taking risks. Preachers who put the articulation of this prophetic imagination at the center of their work—and he makes it clear that preachers don't have to claim to be prophets but should see themselves as "handler[s] of the prophetic tradition"—will most likely encounter intense resistance to the message. The dominant narrative does dominate, after all, and critics are rarely embraced.

Just as the prophets struggled to persuade a royal culture that preferred to ignore the message, so do contemporary preachers need to connect the dots and make a case that goes against the grain. Central to this process is that dot-connecting, that naming of reality.

"Prophetic preaching does not put people in crisis. Rather it names and makes palpable the crisis already pulsing among us," Brueggemann writes. "When the dots are connected, it will require naming the defining sins among us of environmental abuse, neighborly disregard, long-term racism, self-indulgent consumerism, all the staples from those ancient truthtellers translated into our time and place."

This is our task—the tearing down of systems inconsistent with our values and the building up of something new, dismantling and restoration.

What masks those sins, Brueggemann writes, is "a totalizing ideology of exceptionalism that precludes critique of our entitlements and self-regard," and the prophetic imagination helps us see that.

Once we accept this critique of the systems that surround us, the next step is dealing with a sense of loss and the accompanying grief as we let go of the illusions that come with wealth and power. "That function of prophetic preaching is important because in a society of buoyant denial as ours is, there is no venue for public grief," he writes. "It is required, in the dominant narrative, to rush past loss to confident 'recovery' according to a tight ideology of success."

Brueggemann does not suggest we stay mired in grief; when society's denial has been penetrated, prophetic preaching has the task of giving voice to "hope-filled possibility." But he reminds us to be careful not to jump too quickly into an empty hope: "Hope can, of course, be spoken too soon. And when spoken too soon, it may too soon overcome the loss and short-circuit the indispensable embrace of guilt and loss. The new possibility is always on the horizon for prophetic preachers. But good sense and theological courage are required to know when to say what."

Brueggemann's analysis may resonate with many progressive people who aren't churchgoers or don't consider themselves spiritual in any sense.

Christian Values Help Solve Political Problems

This is our task—the tearing down of systems inconsistent with our values and the building up of something new, dismantling and restoration—not only for preachers seeking to be handlers of the prophetic tradition, but for anyone interested in facing honestly our political, economic, and social problems. The task, in Brueggemann's words, is "to mediate a relinquishment of a world that is gone and a reception of a world that is being given."

Again, Brueggemann's goal in the book isn't to advocate for specific politicians, parties, or political programs, but to articulate the underlying values that should inform our political thinking. He seeks to confront truth (against denial) and articulate hope (against despair) in the face of a "denying, despairing, totalizing ideology" that presents itself as the only game in town. While it is difficult for many people to let go of the dominant ideology, Brueggemann argues that people "yearn and trust for more than the empire can offer. We yearn for abundance and transformation and restoration. We yearn beyond the possible."

Brueggemann's analysis may resonate with many progressive people who aren't churchgoers or don't consider themselves spiritual in any sense, but who may ask whether his arguments need to draw on a religious tradition. Wouldn't most of his arguments make just as much sense in the language of secular politics? I think they would, but there is great value in Brueggemann's approach.

Rather than closing down conversation along sectarian lines, our religious traditions have the capacity to open up the conversations about meaning that are difficult to have in a privatized, depoliticized, mass-mediated, mass-medicated world.

First, whatever any one person's beliefs, the dominant religion in the United States is Christianity; around three-quarters of the US population identifies as Christian in some sense. The stories of that tradition are the stories of our culture, and the struggle over that interpretation is crucial to political and social life.

Even more important is the fact that church is still a place where people come to think about these basic questions. Even in the most timid church, the question of "what are people for?" is on the agenda, and hence there is potential to challenge the dominant culture's values.

"The local congregation continues to be a matrix for emancipatory, subversive utterance that is not amenable to totalizing ideology," Brueggemann writes. "People continue to sit and listen attentively to the exposition of the word. People still entertain the odd thought, in spite of the reductionisms of modernity, that God is a real character and the defining agent in the life of the world. People still gather in church to hear and struggle with what is not on offer anywhere else."

Brueggemann's invocation of "God" may put off secular people, who assume that any use of the term implies supernatural claims about God as an actual being that directs the universe. But that is not the only way to understand God, of course. In fact, one of the greatest conversation-starting aspects of this approach is the always provocative question, "What do you mean by God?" When someone cites God, we can—and should—ask: Is God a being, entity, or force in the world? Is God the name humans use for that which is beyond our understanding? What is God to you? Rather than closing down conversation along sectarian lines, our religious traditions have the capacity to open up the conversations about meaning that are difficult to have in a privatized, depoliticized, mass-mediated, mass-medicated world.

To ask whether we should understand our world through a religious or secular lens is to misunderstand both—it's not an either/or proposition. We have the tools of modernity and science to help us understand what we can understand about the material world. We have faith traditions that remind us of the limits of our understanding. In the church I attend (a progressive Presbyterian congregation, St. Andrew's) those two approaches are not at odds but part of the same project—to understand a world facing multiple crises, drawing on the best of religious and secular traditions, struggling together to solve the problems that can be solved and to face the problems that may be beyond solutions.

In a world in collapse, these realities often seem too painful to bear and the work before us often seems overwhelming. The prophetic tradition offers a language for understanding that pain and finding the collective strength to continue.

Religious Fundamentalism Has Transformed Conservative Politics into a Religious Jihad

Neal Gabler

Neal Gabler is a professor, journalist, author, film critic, and po-litical commentator, as well as a senior fellow at the University of Southern California Annenberg Norman Lear Center, a research and public policy organization.

For decades now, liberals have been agonizing because conservatives seem to win even when polls show that the public generally disagrees with them. In their postmortems, liberals have placed blame on the way they frame their message, or on the right-wing media drumbeat that drowns out everything else, or on the right's co-opting of the flag, Mom and apple pie, which is designed to make liberals seem like effete, hostile foreign agents.

It's understandable that liberals prefer to think of their subordination as a matter of their own inadequacies or of conservative wiles. Theoretically, you can learn how to improve your message or how to match wits with adversaries, and a lot of liberal hand-wringing has been dedicated to doing just that. But it is becoming increasingly clear that liberals haven't just been succumbing to superior message control, or even to a superior political narrative (conservatives' frontier individualism versus liberals' communitarianism). They are up against something far more intractable and far more difficult to defeat. They are up against religion.

The Transformation of Conservatism into Religion

Perhaps the single most profound change in our political culture over the last 30 years has been the transformation of conservatism from a political movement, with all the limitations, hedges and forbearances of politics, into a kind of fundamentalist religious movement, with the absolute certainty of religious belief.

I don't mean "religious belief" literally. This transformation is less a function of the alliance between Protestant evangelicals, their fellow travelers and the right (though that alliance has had its effect) than it is a function of a belief in one's own rightness so unshakable that it is not subject to political caveats. In short, what we have in America today is a political fundamentalism, with all the characteristics of religious fundamentalism and very few of the characteristics of politics.

The tea-baggers who hate President Obama . . . honestly believe that the political system . . . is broken and only can be fixed by substituting their certainty for the uncertainties of American politics.

For centuries, American democracy as a process of conflict resolution has been based on give-and-take; negotiation; compromise; the acceptance of the fact that the majority rules, with respect for minority rights; and, above all, on an agreement to abide by the results of a majority vote. It takes compromise, even defeat, in stride because it is a fluid system. As historian Arthur Schlesinger Jr. once put it, the beauty of a democracy is that the minority always has the possibility of becoming the majority.

Religious fundamentalism, on the other hand, rests on immutable truths that cannot be negotiated, compromised or changed. In this, it is diametrically opposed to liberal democracy as we have practiced it in America. Democrats of every political stripe may defend democracy to the death, but very few would defend individual policies to the death. You don't wage bloody crusades for banking regulation or the minimum wage or even healthcare reform. When politics becomes religion, however, policy too becomes a matter of life and death, as we have all seen.

That is one reason our founding fathers opted for a separation of church and state. They recognized that religion and politics could coexist only when they occupied different domains. Most denominations, which preach and practice tolerance, have rendered unto Caesar what is Caesar's. Religious groups may have found a community of interest with a political party to further their aims; they have not, by and large, sought to convert the political system into a religious one. Until now.

You cannot convince religious fanatics of anything other than what they already believe, even if their religion is political dogma.

The tea-baggers who hate President [Barack] Obama with a fervor that is beyond politics; the fear-mongers who warn that Obama is another Hitler or Stalin; the wannabe storm troopers who brandish their guns and warn darkly of the president's demise; the cable and talk-radio blowhards who make a living out of demonizing Obama and tarring liberals as America-haters—these people are not just exercising their rights within the political system. They honestly believe that the political system—a system that elected Obama—is broken and only can be fixed by substituting their certainty for the uncertainties of American politics.

A Losing Battle

As we are sadly discovering, this minority cannot be headed off, which is most likely why conservatism transmogrified from politics to a religion in the first place. Conservatives who sincerely believed that theirs is the only true and right path have come to realize that political tolerance is no match for religious vehemence.

Unfortunately, they are right. Having opted out of political discourse, they are not susceptible to any suasion. Rationality won't work because their arguments are faith-based rather than evidence-based. Better message control won't work. Improved strategies won't work. Grass-roots organizing won't work. Nothing will work because you cannot convince religious fanatics of anything other than what they already believe, even if their religion is political dogma.

And therein lies the problem, not only for liberals but for mainstream conservatives who think of conservatism as an ideology, not an orthodoxy. You cannot beat religion with politics, which is why the extreme right "wins" so many battles. The fundamentalist political fanatics will always be more zealous than mainstream conservatives or liberals. They will always be louder, more adamant, more aggrieved, more threatening, more willing to do anything to win. Losing is inconceivable. For them, every battle is a crusade—or a jihad—a matter of good and evil.

There is something terrifying in this. The media have certainly been cowed; they treat intolerance as if it were legitimate political activity. So have many politicians, and not just the conservative ones who know that if they don't fall in line, they will be run over. This political fundamentalism has also invaded the general culture in deleterious ways. The ugly incivility of recent months is partly the result of political fundamentalists who have nothing but contempt for opposing viewpoints, which gives them license to shout down opponents or threaten them, just as jihadis everywhere do.

Those who oppose the religification of politics may think all they have to do is change tactics, but they are sadly, tragically mistaken. They can never win, because for the political fundamentalists, this isn't political jousting, this is Armageddon.

With stakes like that, they will not lose, and there is nothing democrats—small 'd' and capital "D"—can do about it.

What Role Should Religion Play in Politics, Judicial Decisions and Laws?

Brian Faller

Brian Faller is an attorney and a member of the board of contributors for The Olympian, *a newspaper in Olympia, Washington.*

Is it appropriate that judges, politicians or voters make decisions and publicly justify those decisions based on religious texts?

For example, would it be objectionable that passages from the Bible or the Quran serve as a legal justification for laws that criminalize abortion?

The United States Constitution provides for a separation of church and state. It prohibits laws "respecting an establishment of religion" and laws applying a religious test for eligibility to hold a public office. At the same time, the Constitution secures the "free exercise" of religion so that people can believe and practice (or not) a faith of their choice.

This separation of church and state protects the citizen from having the religious views of others imposed on them by coercive law or by legislation of a religious concept of the good. It thus protects a pluralism of religions and moral views against theocracy and the civil strife it leads to when government enforces a religion on unwilling citizens.

The doctrine of separation also reflects the fact that religious beliefs are traditionally based upon asserted revealed truths that a significant segment of other believers and nonbelievers reasonably do not accept as reliable sources or truths.

Indeed, religious followers often interpret the same religious texts to reach vastly different conclusions, and in modern society, numerous commands in religious books such as stoning prostitutes to death, amputating hands of thieves, and beating disobedient children, are proscribed.

Clearly citizens (and politicians) are free under our Constitution to argue for laws based on religion and could not be punished for doing so. However, the question here is not one of legal duty, but of a civic duty which is an ideal not enforceable by law, like the duty to vote.

If politicians and citizens publicly accept religious justifications for law, the pressure would mount for judges (who are appointed by politicians or elected by citizens) to follow.

Many political philosophers argue that to preserve pluralistic democracy, citizens and politicians should recognize a civic duty to base their votes and public justification of coercive laws on neutral grounds, such as shared values and factual considerations, rather than revealed religious truths or one's comprehensive moral view. Such a view does not exclude values found in religion or moral theory from the public debate where such values are shared among reasonable persons.

The abortion dispute can provide an example how neutral grounds work. The public abortion debate might be recast in non-religious terms, shifting the focus from a religious designation of an embryo/early fetus as a person or human being to considerations of fact, such as whether and to what extent an embryo/early fetus has thoughts, memories, expectations, a sense of loss, differentiates self from world, acts, experiences pain from abortion, resembles a human, etc., whether and to what extent our shared values give moral weight to the potential of an organism to develop characteristics of mature humans, whether and to what extent prohibition will result in deaths of mothers from illegal abortions and in childbirth, whether and to what extent children who would have been aborted will be adequately cared for, whether and to what extent allowing abortion will lead to societal acceptance of infanticide, euthanasia, or mistreatment of humans with mental or physical challenges, etc.

No doubt I have left off a number of important considerations in the abortion debate, but this list illustrates how controversial issues can at least in part be addressed by identifying and weighing factual outcomes and shared values.

Indeed, neutral grounds are themselves used to justify this civic duty. If politicians and citizens publicly accept religious justifications for law, the pressure would mount for judges (who are appointed by politicians or elected by citizens) to follow. And if politicians and citizens publicly justify their votes on nonreligious grounds but actually vote based on religious grounds, it would at times result in hypocritical laws silently justified on religious grounds.

To me, these considerations suggest that we should recognize a civic duty to base our votes and public justifications of coercive laws on neutral, nonreligious grounds, because doing so provides a critical bulwark to safeguard pluralistic democracy from creeping theocracy.

A Majority of Americans Think Churches Should Stay Out of Politics

The Pew Forum on Religion & Public Life

The Pew Forum on Religion & Public Life is a project of the Pew Research Center, a nonpartisan research and polling organization that provides information on the issues, attitudes, and trends affecting the United States and the world.

A new survey finds signs of public uneasiness with the mixing of religion and politics. The number of people who say there has been too much religious talk by political leaders stands at an all-time high since the Pew Research Center began asking the question more than a decade ago. And most Americans continue to say that churches and other houses of worship should keep out of politics.

Survey Results

Nearly four-in-ten Americans (38%) now say there has been too much expression of religious faith and prayer from political leaders, while 30% say there has been too little. In 2010, more said there was too little than too much religious expression from politicians (37% vs. 29%). The percentage saying there is too much expression of religious faith by politicians has increased across party lines, but this view remains far more widespread among Democrats than Republicans.

Slightly more than half of the public (54%) says that churches should keep out of politics, compared with 40% who

This is an excerpt from the report "More See 'Too Much' Religious Talk by Politicians" by the *Pew Research Center's Forum on Religion & Public Life*. See http://www.pewforum.org/politics-and-elections/more-see-too-much-religious-talk-by-politicians.aspx for graphics, tables and information about how the survey was conducted. © 2012, Pew Research Center. http://pewforum.org/.

say religious institutions should express their views on social and political matters. This is the third consecutive poll conducted over the past four years in which more people have said churches and other houses of worship should keep out of politics than said they should express their views on social and political topics. By contrast, between 1996 and 2006 the balance of opinion on this question consistently tilted in the opposite direction.

These are among the findings from the latest national survey by the Pew Research Center for the People & the Press and the Pew Research Center's Forum on Religion & Public Life, conducted March 7–11 among 1,503 adults. While there are substantial partisan differences over religion and politics, the survey finds there also are divisions within the GOP [Republican] primary electorate.

51% of the public say that religious conservatives have too much control over the Republican Party.

Nearly six-in-ten (57%) Republican and Republican-leaning voters who favor Mitt Romney for the Republican nomination say churches should keep out of political matters. By contrast, 60% of GOP voters who support Rick Santorum say that churches and other houses of worship should express their views on social and political questions.

And while 55% of Santorum's supporters say there is too little expression of religious faith and prayer by political leaders, just 24% of Romney's backers agree, while 33% say there is too much expression of faith and prayer by politicians.

The new survey finds that more people view the GOP as friendly to religion than say the same about the Democratic Party, a pattern observed for much of the past decade.

At the same time, 51% of the public say that religious conservatives have too much control over the Republican

Party. Fewer express the view that liberals who are not religious have too much control over the Democratic Party (41%).

Opinions about whether the [Barack] Obama administration is friendly toward religion have shifted modestly since 2009. Currently, 39% say the administration is friendly to religion, 32% say it is neutral and 23% say it is unfriendly. The balance of opinion was comparable in August 2009, although somewhat fewer (17%) said the administration was unfriendly to religion.

However, there has been a noticeable shift in opinions among white Catholics, perhaps reflecting effects from the controversy over the administration's policies on contraception coverage. The percentage of white Catholics who say the administration is unfriendly to religion has nearly doubled—from 17% to 31%—since 2009. Three years ago, far more white Catholics said the administration was friendly (35%) than unfriendly to religion (17%); today, nearly as many say the administration is unfriendly (31%) as friendly (38%).

Expressions of Faith by Political Leaders

A plurality of the public (38%) says that there has been too much expression of religious faith and prayer from political leaders, while 30% say there has been too little religious expression and 25% say there has been the right amount of discussion of religion from political leaders. The number saying there has been too much religious talk from political leaders now stands at its highest point since the Pew Research Center began asking the question more than a decade ago.

Since October 2001, shortly after the 9/11 attacks, the rise in the number saying there has been too much religious expression by political leaders has been most pronounced among Democrats and independents. Nearly half of Democrats (46%) now say there has been too much discussion of religious faith and prayer by politicians, as do 42% of independents.

The number of Republicans expressing unease with the amount of politicians' religious talk also has increased (from 8% in 2001 to 24% currently). But Republicans have consistently been less inclined than either Democrats or independents to say there has been too much religious talk from political leaders.

Since 2010, there have been sizable increases in the percentages of white mainline Protestants, white Catholics and the religiously unaffiliated saying that there has been too much discussion of religion by political leaders.

However, there has been no change in opinions among white evangelical Protestants, who remain far less likely than those in other religious groups to say that politicians express religious faith too much.

Roughly half of college graduates (49%) now say there has been too much religious discussion from political leaders, up 14 points since 2010. Those with some college education have also become increasingly uncomfortable with the amount of religious expression from political leaders, with 38% now saying there has been too much religion talk from politicians (up from 27% in 2010). By contrast, there has been little change in opinion on this question among those with a high school degree or less education.

White evangelical Protestants . . . remain far less likely than those in other religious groups to say that politicians express religious faith too much.

Views of Churches' Involvement in Politics

A majority of Americans (54%) say that churches and other houses of worship should keep out of political matters, while 40% say they should express their views on social and political questions. After a decade in which the balance of opinion tilted in the opposite direction, this is the third consecutive survey in the past four years in which more people say churches should keep out of politics than say churches should express their views on social and political issues.

When this question was first asked by the Pew Research Center in 1996, there was little partisan division. Roughly four-in-ten Republicans and independents said churches should keep out of politics (42% each), as did 44% of Democrats. Currently, 44% of Republicans say churches should stay out of politics, compared with 60% of Democrats and 58% of independents.

Majorities of the religiously unaffiliated . . . say churches and other houses of worship should steer clear of politics.

There also are significant divisions on this issue among religious groups. A majority of white evangelical Protestants (60%) say that churches and other houses of worship should express their views on social and political issues. The views of this group have changed little since 2006, even as the public as a whole has increasingly taken the view that religious institutions should keep out of politics.

Black Protestants are divided on this question, with 51% saying churches should express their views and 43% saying they should keep out of politics. By contrast, in July 2006, 69% of black Protestants said churches and other houses of worship should express their views on social and political issues.

Majorities of the religiously unaffiliated (66%), Catholics (60%) and white mainline Protestants (60%) say churches and other houses of worship should steer clear of politics.

Political Parties' Friendliness to Religion

A majority of the public (54%) views the Republican Party as friendly to religion, while 24% say the GOP is neutral to religion and 13% say it is unfriendly toward religion. Roughly four-in-ten (39%) rate the Obama administration as friendly, with 32% saying it is neutral and 23% saying the administration is unfriendly to religion. The Democratic Party is seen as friendly to religion by 35% of the public; it is seen as neutral by 36% and as unfriendly by 21% of the public.

Approximately one-in-five Americans (19%) rate news reporters and the news media as friendly to religion, and 14% say university professors are friendly to religion. Roughly one-in-three say that reporters (35%) and professors (32%) are unfriendly to religion.

Over the past decade, the Republican Party has consistently been seen as friendly to religion by more people than has the Democratic Party. The current poll finds a significant rebound since 2010 in the number describing both parties as friendly to religion.

The increase in the percentage viewing the GOP as friendly to religion has been broad-based. Nearly two-thirds of Republicans (65%) describe the GOP as friendly to religion, up eight points since 2010, as do roughly half (54%) of political independents, up 12 points. Among Democrats, 48% now view the GOP as friendly to religion, compared with 36% who said this in 2010.

The number of people saying the Obama administration is friendly to religion is steady compared with 2009.

The rise in the number saying the Democratic Party is friendly to religion is concentrated among Democrats and independents. A clear majority of Democrats (57%) now view their party as friendly to religion, up 15 points since 2010. The percentage of independents describing the Democratic Party as friendly to religion now stands at 29%, up from 20% in 2010.

The Obama Administration and Religion

A plurality of the public (39%) says the Obama administration is friendly to religion, while 32% say the administration is neutral toward religion and 23% say it is unfriendly to religion. A majority of Democrats (59%) say the administration is friendly to religion, while about half of Republicans polled say it is unfriendly toward religion. Independents are evenly divided between those who view the administration as friendly to religion (36%) and those who see it as neutral toward religion (38%); 21% of independents see the Obama administration as unfriendly to religion.

These partisan leanings are reflected in the views of religious groups. A plurality of white evangelicals (44%) views the administration as unfriendly toward religion, while two-thirds of black Protestants (65%) say it is friendly toward religion.

The number of people saying the Obama administration is friendly to religion is steady compared with 2009, when this question was last asked. But over the same period of time, there has been a small but noticeable increase in the number saying the Obama administration is unfriendly to religion (from 17% in 2009 to 23% today). This change is concentrated exclusively among Republicans, among whom half (52%) now view the Obama administration as unfriendly to religion.

The number of Catholics describing the Obama administration as unfriendly to religion has risen 10-percentage points since 2009 (from 15% to 25%); among white Catholics, roughly one-third (31%) now view the administration as unfriendly to religion, up 14 points since 2009. There also has been a significant increase in the percentage of the religiously unaffiliated who view the Obama administration as unfriendly to religion.

Reporters, Professors, and Religion

About a third of the public (32%) perceives university professors as unfriendly to religion, while 37% describe professors as neutral to religion; far fewer (14%) say university professors are generally friendly toward religion. Compared with 2003 (when this question was last asked), there has been a noticeable rise in the number describing professors as unfriendly to religion and a slight downturn in the number saying professors are friendly to religion.

College graduates are more apt than those with less education to describe professors as neutral toward religion, while more of those who have not graduated from college express no opinion on this question.

A majority of Republicans (56%) say that professors are unfriendly toward religion. By contrast, a plurality of Democrats (46%) says that professors are neutral toward religion. Among independents, 37% say professors are neutral toward religion, while 31% describe them as unfriendly and 16% say they are friendly to religion.

Among white evangelicals surveyed, 56% view professors as unfriendly toward religion. Among most other religious groups, pluralities or majorities describe professors as either neutral or friendly toward religion.

Independents, by a wide margin . . . say that religious conservatives have too much influence over the GOP.

Roughly a third (35%) of the public says that news reporters and the news media are unfriendly toward religion, while 38% describe reporters as neutral to religion and 19% describe the media as friendly toward religion. The number saying news reporters are friendly toward religion has increased slightly compared with 2009, whereas the number describing the media as neutral toward religion has ticked down since then.

A majority of Republicans (56%) see the media as un-friendly to religion, while most Democrats and independents say reporters are neutral or friendly to religion. About half of white evangelicals in the survey (53%) say reporters and the news media are unfriendly toward religion. Among other religious groups, half or more rate the news media as neutral or friendly to religion.

Religious Conservatives Seen as Having Too Much Control over GOP

About half of the public (51%) agrees that religious conservatives have too much control over the GOP. Fewer (41%) agree that liberals who are not religious have too much control over the Democratic Party. These opinions are little changed from August 2008, during the last presidential campaign.

Partisans break along predictable lines in views of the influences over their own party and the opposing party. Independents, by a wide margin (57% to 42%), are more likely than to say that religious conservatives have too much influence over the GOP than that secular liberals have too much sway over the Democratic Party.

The religiously unaffiliated stand out as the religious group most inclined to think that religious conservatives have too much sway in the GOP, with 66% expressing this view. Roughly half of white mainline Protestants (53%) and white Catholics (56%) say the same. By contrast, 56% of white evangelicals disagree that religious conservatives have too much power in the GOP.

The belief that secular liberals have too much control over the Democratic Party is most pronounced among white evangelicals (58%). White mainline Protestants, white Catholics and black Protestants are divided on this question, while the large majority of the religiously unaffiliated (64%) rejects the idea that secular liberals have too much power over the Democratic Party.

CHAPTER 2

Does Government Interfere with Religious Freedom?

Chapter Preface

One of the persistent myths about the United States is that it has always been a land of religious tolerance. Presidents from George Washington to Barack Obama have lauded the country's commitment to religious freedom, its embrace of all religious beliefs, and its secular government. The truth is a very different story, one of religious persecution of minority religions, battles among various religious sects, animosity toward unbelievers and native religions, and governmental sanctions of favored religions.

Many Americans are familiar with the history of the Puritans who fled religious persecution in England and established settlements in North America in the 1600s, but this well-known story is only part of the country's early history. Although the Puritans experienced persecution themselves and saw its injustice, they mostly failed to treat other religions with the tolerance or acceptance they sought for themselves. Certain of their faith, the Puritans made their chosen religious beliefs the foundation of their communities' civic government. Believers in other religions, like Catholics or Quakers, were banned from Puritan settlements in the Boston area, and in some cases these individuals were attacked or hanged for asserting their religious beliefs.

The local and state governments that formed in early North America also favored some religions over others and discriminated against certain religious groups. In Massachusetts, for example, Catholics were forbidden from holding public office unless they renounced their loyalty to the pope. Similarly, New York State's constitution initially banned Catholics from public office, and other states such as Maryland approved of Catholics but not Jews. A number of states also had state-sanctioned and state-supported churches. Even Virginia, home of founding father Thomas Jefferson, considered legislation that would have linked the state government with Christian religions, but this step was avoided when the state legislature instead passed Jefferson's plan calling for freedom of religion and separation of church and state.

Thomas Jefferson's vision of religious freedom and tolerance eventually became part of the 1776 US Constitution. Article VI provides that no religious test can ever be required as a qualification for any public office, and the First Amendment contains a guarantee of religious freedom and a prohibition against government establishment of religion. However, these constitutional protections were violated in the years that followed.

Beginning in the colonial period, for example, Catholics experienced many forms of discrimination, including legislation that limited their rights and freedoms. Catholics were often barred from public office, excluded from certain professions, denied voting rights, and prevented from owning land or property. In some cases, parents were fined for sending their children to Catholic schools. Prejudice against Catholics slowly subsided in the United States in the modern era, but it was still a factor in 1960 when John F. Kennedy, a Catholic, ran for president.

Similarly, during the nineteenth and much of the twentieth centuries, Jews were routinely discriminated against in employment, schools, social clubs, and other arenas. Anti-Semitism peaked in the 1920s and 1930s and then slowly waned after World War II, after millions of Jews immigrated to the United States from Eastern Europe and, like other immigrant groups, gradually integrated into US society and the US economy.

Mormons, too, were persecuted by many Americans, especially in the nineteenth century, when acts of violence were sometimes directed against Mormon communities. In Missouri, for example, following a battle between Mormons and the state militia, Governor Lilburn Boggs in 1833 issued an extermination order, forcing Mormons to leave the state. The Mormon sect also met opposition in Illinois, where its founder Joseph Smith was murdered. Eventually, Mormons settled in what is now Utah. Times have changed significantly since the 1800s, but Mitt Romney, a Mormon presidential candidate in the 2012 presidential election, nevertheless found his faith to be a topic of much interest and debate.

In the early 2000s, Muslims living in the United States came under attack, following the terrorist attacks of September 11, 2001. Moreover, the focus on terrorists who follow a militant or radical form of Islam caused many American Christians to see all Muslims as violent extremists. Peaceful American Muslims have suffered as a result, enduring hate speech, suspicions that they are terrorists, and attacks on their mosques. In 2010, a controversy began over the building of an Islamic community center in New York City near Ground Zero, the location of the World Trade Center buildings that were targeted by terrorists on 9/11. Protests erupted around the United States, and many argued that Muslims should not be permitted to build the center so close to the memorial site because it would disrespect the people killed in the attack. The controversy eased after New York mayor Michael Bloomberg and President Barack Obama stood up for the rights of Muslims, and the Islamic center opened quietly in September 2011.

This trend of Islamophobia coincides with the insistence among various Christian groups that the federal government infringes on their religious freedom. The authors of the viewpoints included in this chapter discuss whether the United States and other governments are interfering with religious freedom.

President Barack Obama's Health Insurance Mandate Violates the Religious Beliefs of Catholic Institutions

Mike Brownfield

Mike Brownfield is assistant director of strategic communications at The Heritage Foundation, a conservative think tank, and he is editor of The Foundry, *Heritage's public policy news blog, and* The Morning Bell, *the group's e-newsletter.*

It has not even been two years since Obamacare was enacted, and already the President's health care law has taken another victim—the religious freedoms Americans hold dear, as reflected by the First Amendment.

The Contraception Rule

The [Barack] Obama Administration recently reaffirmed a rule under Obamacare that requires many religious employers to provide health care coverage for all FDA [Food and Drug Administration]-approved contraceptive methods, sterilization procedures, and related education and counseling. On the grounds that certain FDA-approved contraceptive methods can sometimes "cause the demise of embryos both after and before uterine implantation," many groups also believe that the rule forces them to cover abortion.

The United States Conference of Catholic Bishops is calling the contraception mandate an "unprecedented" attack on religious freedom. And in statement after statement issued in diocese after diocese, many bishops are publicly declaring that they "cannot" and "will not" comply with "this unjust law." As Cleveland Bishop Richard Lennon explained, "Unless this rule is overturned, Catholics will be compelled either to violate our consciences or to drop health care coverage for our employees."

The Obama Administration has imposed its will on the very institutions the First Amendment sought to protect.

It's not just Catholics affected by the rule, however. Leaders from other faith traditions have expressed their concern, and the Becket Fund for Religious Liberty has already filed a lawsuit on behalf of an interdenominational Christian college that objects to providing abortion and related education and counseling in its health care insurance. "The mandate is un-American, unprecedented, and flagrantly unconstitutional," says an attorney for the college.

As shocking as the Obama Administration's action is, it should not come as a surprise. Heritage [Foundation] experts explained years ago that freedom of conscience in health care is closely linked to greater personal freedom over health care decisions. Health care expert James Capretta says that "it was inevitable—only a matter of time," now that the government is calling the shots and making health care choices for the American people. "Just the sight of Catholic leaders' being forced to go begging before federal officials ought to be enough to convince most Americans that handing over so much power over such sensitive matters to the federal government was a terrible, terrible mistake," he writes.

This erosion of fundamental religious freedoms at the hands of the Obamacare bureaucracy is the sort of clash of government versus religious freedom that the Founders foresaw when, in the First Amendment of the Constitution, they prescribed that "Congress shall make no law respecting an establishment of religion, or prohibiting the free exercise thereof." Not withstanding that prohibition, the Obama Administration has imposed its will on the very institutions the First Amendment sought to protect. Though the rule provides a narrow exemption for "houses of worship," it unfortunately burdens their affiliated institutions, schools, and hospitals—thereby violating the freedom of religion. David Addington, Vice President of Domestic and Economic Policy at The Heritage Foundation, explains that the Obama Administration should take action to exempt these institutions and preserve their religious liberty:

> The Department of Health and Human Services should broadly exempt religious institutions in its final regulations implementing the Obamacare contraception mandate, pending repeal of that mandate as part of the Obamacare statute repeal. Such an exemption would allow the religious institutions both to adhere, as they must, to the tenets of their faiths and to provide group health care plans for their employees. Absent such an exemption, many religious institutions, following their faiths, will have no alternative but to stop making group health plans available to their employees and pay any fines for failure to do so.
>
> Surely President Obama did not intend what he considers his signature legislative achievement to trample on freedom of religion and to result in the loss of group health care coverage for employees of religious institutions. This is, after all, the man who told us all in 2006 that "secularists are wrong when they ask believers to leave their religion at the door before entering into the public square."

New York Archbishop Timothy Dolan cautioned, "This latest erosion of our first freedom should make all Americans pause. When the government tampers with a freedom so fundamental to the life of our nation, one shudders to think what lies ahead." Those dire words of warning sadly ring true. Obamacare was designed to place total power in the hands of the federal government—in an unelected bureaucracy with the power to dictate the operation of an industry that is fundamental to Americans' health and wellbeing. With this decision, the Obama Administration has demonstrated just how far that power can go, what freedoms it can take away, and why this law must be repealed.

The US Government Has Taken a Number of Actions That Restrict Religious Freedom

Sarah Pulliam Bailey

Sarah Pulliam Bailey is the online editor for Christianity Today, *a religious magazine.*

The past year [2011] has marked a shift in religious liberty debates, one that previously centered on hiring rights but became focused on health care requirements. When President [Barack] Obama first took office [January 2009], faith-based groups were especially concerned that organizations that discriminate in hiring based on religious beliefs would become ineligible for federal funding. In 2011, the President indicated that he would not rescind an executive order on hiring rights. Just a week later, though, Health and Human Services ruled that religious groups other than churches must provide their employees contraception, triggering lawsuits and petitions. But contraception is not the only religious freedom issue faith-based groups are eyeing. The following timeline shows a number of actions the government took in the past year, setting precedents and priorities on various issues, including sexual orientation, health care, and hiring decisions.

Health care workers and the 'conscience clause'

February 18, 2011: The Obama administration revises "conscience clause" rules, maintaining the provision that allows workers to refrain from performing abortions but calling the Bush-enacted rule "unclear and potentially overbroad in scope." The earlier provision was interpreted as allowing such workers to opt out of a broad range of medical services, such as providing Plan B or other contraception.

Defense of Marriage Act

February 23, 2011: President Obama announced that the federal government would no longer defend the constitutionality of the Defense of Marriage Act. The move stemmed from the administration's decision that sexual orientation should be protected by the highest legal scrutiny afforded by the 14th Amendment. Neither the Supreme Court nor federal law has added sexual orientation to the list of characteristics especially protected against discrimination, like race, gender, or national origin. But the administration's efforts to add it could set a precedent. Many observers believe such an inclusion would allow the government to invoke a "compelling government interest" in forbidding faith-based organizations from considering some sexual ethics questions in employment decisions.

Prisons

April 13, 2011: The Justice Department files a lawsuit against a county in South Carolina where a South Carolina sheriff was prohibiting inmates from getting devotional materials. The county eventually agreed to let inmates receive religious materials.

National Day of Prayer and courts

April 14, 2011: A federal appeals court dismisses a lawsuit against the National Day of Prayer, overturning a 2010 U.S. District ruling that the day was unconstitutional, which the Justice Department appealed. Obama had discontinued President Bush's annual observances at the White House, but issued a proclamation on the 2011 National Day of Prayer.

Hiring rights and federal funding

July 25, 2011: Comments from President Obama suggested that he does not plan to change an executive order that permits some faith-based organizations that receive federal funding to discriminate in hiring based on applicants' religious beliefs. Obama maintained a position in an executive order that states that while federally-funded religious organizations cannot discriminate against beneficiaries, they may retain religious hiring practices.

Contraception and religious exemption

August 1, 2011: The Department of Health and Human Services announced that employers must provide contraceptives (including those that block uterine implantation) in insurance plans. Churches are exempt from the mandate, but not religious employers, such as soup kitchens, homeless shelters, parachurch ministries, religious hospitals, and religious universities. The ruling triggers petitions and requests for a stronger religious exemption, including a lawsuit from Colorado Christian University.

Chaplains and 'Don't Ask Don't Tell'

September 20, 2011: The military ended its "don't ask, don't tell" policy on gays and lesbians serving openly in the military. The Pentagon also issued a memo allowing military chaplains to perform same-sex marriages if it is allowed by the law and the chaplain's beliefs.

The United States Agency for International Development (USAID) began inserting new language in its mandatory requirements, saying that it "strongly encourages" all grant applicants to adopt USAID's hiring policy of not discriminating on the basis of sexual orientation.

Hiring rights and discrimination

October 5, 2011: As the Supreme Court considered *Hosanna-Tabor v. EEOC*, an employment dispute at a Lutheran school, the administration argued that the First Amendment's religion clauses do not exempt churches from employment discrimination laws, even when considering head clergy. (Though the administration did allow that the right of expressive association might be compromised by such laws.)

In January 2012, a unanimous Court rejected the administration's argument as untenable, saying, "We cannot accept the remarkable view that the Religion Clauses have nothing to say about a religious organization's freedom to select its own ministers."

Hiring rights and sexual orientation

October 11, 2011: The United States Agency for International Development (USAID) began inserting new language in its mandatory requirements, saying that it "strongly encourages" all grant applicants to adopt USAID's hiring policy of not discriminating on the basis of sexual orientation. Christian aid groups like World Vision opposed the language and unsuccessfully asked for additional language clarifying that religious employers retain rights to consider religion in hiring. USAID says the policy is not binding and White House officials suggest dialogue on the issue will continue.

Federal funding and sex trafficking

October 2011: Health and Human Services [HHS] defunded the U.S. Conference of Catholic Bishops' [USCCB] domestic program to assist and resettle human trafficking victims. More than 20 U.S. senators wrote a letter to HHS requesting an explanation. The USCCB believes its program was defunded because of its religious opposition to providing abortions or contraceptives to trafficked women.

Discrimination and hiring rights

December 6, 2011: President Obama issued a memorandum announcing that ending discrimination against those who are gay "is central to the United States commitment to promoting human rights" and "directing all agencies engaged abroad to ensure that U.S. diplomacy and foreign assistance promote and protect the human rights of LGBT [lesbian, gay, bisexual, and trangendered] persons." On December 16, a dozen faith-based groups who engage in international relief and development sent a private letter to Obama, urging him to clarify to agencies that his directive does not affect religious organizations' hiring rights. The letter asked him to clarify that his memo would not mandate a new LGBT "litmus test" for indigenous groups that the organizations partner with in international relief work. The White House did not reply to the group's letter.

Contraception and national security

December 19, 2011: President Obama signed an executive order declaring women's access to reproductive healthcare during conflict and humanitarian emergencies a matter of U.S. national security. It is unclear whether the declaration will be cited as evidence that there would be a compelling government interest in compelling federal grantees to distribute emergency contraceptives that block uterine implantation.

Contraception and religious exemption

January 20, 2012: Health and Human Services announced that it will not expand the religious exemption for the August contraception ruling beyond churches, sparking further concern from religious groups. Secretary Kathleen Sebelius extends the enforcement of the mandate to 2013.

Contraception and cost

February 10, 2012: President Obama announced that insurers will be responsible for paying for contraceptives, raising questions about self-insured religious groups. The ruling did not expand the religious conscience exemption to faith-based groups other than churches. Pro-life groups suggest insurance companies could raise premiums to cover the cost of contraception. The White House suggests that the policy would not allow insurers to raise premiums due to contraception.

A cross and establishment of religion

March 14, 2012: The Obama administration filed a brief with the Supreme Court in opposition to the U.S. 9th Circuit Court of Appeals' 3-0 ruling that declared a 43-foot-tall cross that serves as a war memorial on Mt. Soledad in San Diego was an unconstitutional establishment of religion. The brief states, "The decision . . . if permitted to stand, calls for the government to tear down a memorial cross that has stood for 58 years as a tribute to fallen service members. Nothing in the Establishment Clause compels that result."

Administering contraception

March 16, 2012: The Obama administration proposed further recommendations for its earlier ruling on contraception. The proposal does not expand the religious conscience exemption, specifying that the ruling would not set a precedent for future laws. The proposal suggests that a third-party administrator of the group health plan or another independent entity would assume responsibility for the contraception coverage for self-insured organizations. The final regulation will be implemented August 2013.

Religious Freedom Under Assault

Thomas S. Kidd

Thomas S. Kidd is an author and a senior fellow at Baylor University's Institute for Studies of Religion.

The next time you walk into church, or your synagogue or mosque, say a little thanks to God for our founding principles. There's a lot for which to be grateful, after all, and the freedom to worship is among our greatest blessings.

But a new report by Pew Research Center's Forum on Religion & Public Life has revealed a disturbing pattern: Nearly a third of the globe's population—2.2 billion people—live in countries where religious persecution *increased* between 2006 and 2009.

Observers have often assumed that over time, the world would progress toward what political scientist Francis Fukuyama famously called "the end of history," when Western liberal democracy would triumph over all ideological competitors. But instead, we are seeing a marked erosion of what America's Founding Fathers considered the "first freedom": the liberty of religious conscience. Even in America, there are signs that our historic commitment to this freedom is wavering.

The countries with the largest populations in the world, India and China, are among the worst offenders in social harassment or government restrictions on religion. No surprise, there. In China, the government commonly imprisons dissidents, ranging from those of the Falun Gong spiritual movement to pastors of Christian house churches. Even now, Beijing authorities are seeking to shut down the evangelical Shouwang Church, which has dared to hold outdoor assemblies.

Christians Being Targeted

In the Middle East, the "Arab Spring" has not been auspicious for religious liberty. The uprisings against repressive governments have precipitated a treacherous new era for the region's Christian minorities. According to the Pew report, Egypt was already the world's largest country with rising levels of government restrictions on religion before the ouster of Hosni Mubarak; since then, the situation has grown even worse.

Christians in the U.S. take their lumps, too, when it comes to religious freedom. These range from the frivolous . . . to real judicial infringements.

In the past six months, appalling religious violence has convulsed Egypt, especially against its Coptic Christians. Rumors about a Coptic convert to Islam being held against her will led to vicious rioting on May 8, leaving 15 dead, 200 injured, and churches looted and burned. This was only one in a series of anti-Christian incidents that has respected Middle East journalist Yasmine El Rashidi warning of an Islamist takeover in Egypt. In the Pew report, Muslim-dominated countries tended to have both high government restrictions and social pressures against religious freedom.

And what about in the USA? You won't see the kind of religious persecution here as in other parts of the world, but religious freedom is taking its hits. This is not a problem rooted exclusively in the political left or right, either.

As one might expect, some Muslims in America have faced persistent harassment since 9/11. Opponents have attempted legal measures to stop the construction of Muslim worship sites, from the controversial (and, I would argue, unnecessarily provocative) Islamic center at Ground Zero, to a neighborhood mosque in Murfreesboro, Tenn. Certain Republican leaders, such as Herman Cain, have proposed loyalty oaths for Muslims serving in government. Really. Overall, the FBI reports that more than 1,500 religious hate crimes occur annually, although the majority target Jews.

But Christians in the U.S. take their lumps, too, when it comes to religious freedom. These range from the frivolous— such as a recent (and unsuccessful) Freedom from Religion Foundation lawsuit to ban Texas Gov. Rick Perry from holding "The Response," his prayer rally in Houston—to real judicial infringements.

Freedom and the Courts

Earlier this month, for instance, a federal appeals court approved San Diego State University's policy of denying a Christian sorority and fraternity official campus benefits simply because the groups restricted membership to Christians.

And in October, the U.S. Supreme Court will hear oral arguments in what might become the most significant religious liberty case in decades, *Hosanna-Tabor Church v. EEOC*, which will, disconcertingly, consider whether a religious school has the right to fire a teacher who contradicts official church teachings.

Should the court rule against Hosanna-Tabor, it could indicate that American courts will intrude more and more upon the internal affairs of religious organizations, dictating that the right to free exercise must bow before judges' and bureaucrats' current conceptions of legal equity. Placing religious groups under special legal disadvantages, and forbidding them from operating according to their own beliefs, is certainly not what the Founders had in mind when they banned an "establishment of religion" in the First Amendment.

Let's hope that, instead, America will renew its commitment to the genius of the First Amendment's religion clauses.

The government should never promote the interests of any one faith—including secularism—but should protect the free exercise of religion for all.

In light of the Pew report, the world needs our example more than ever.

Obama's Defense of Religion

Steve Chapman

Steve Chapman is a blogger and a member of the editorial board of the Chicago Tribune.

Catholic bishops, evangelical pastors and Republican presidential candidates have been decrying the Obama administration's war on religious liberty. Amid all the uproar, it's easy to overlook something equally important: the administration's many battles *for* religious liberty.

The president has gotten deserved criticism for trying to force Catholic colleges and hospitals to buy insurance coverage for something they regard as evil: birth control. But that's only part of the story. In other realms, believers have found Barack Obama and his Justice Department to be staunch allies.

The most conspicuous surprise involves government rules for faith-based organizations that get federal funding for social services. President George W. Bush issued an executive order allowing such groups to hire only people who share their faith—exempting them from the usual ban on religious discrimination. Liberal critics accused him of underwriting "theocracy" and "faith-based coercion."

One of the opponents was Obama. In his presidential campaign, he said his view was simple: "If you get a federal grant, you can't use that grant money to proselytize to the people you help and you can't discriminate against them—or against the people you hire—on the basis of their religion."

But it hasn't worked out that way. Obama has left Bush's rule in place, infuriating many groups that expected a reversal.

They have repeatedly pressed him to bar these groups from using religious criteria in deciding whom to hire and whom to serve. Last year, the Coalition Against Religious Discrimination wrote the White House complaining that "we have seen no forward movement on this issue."

That's not the sentiment at the Institutional Religious Freedom Alliance, which includes such perennial Obama critics as the U.S. Conference of Catholic Bishops, Focus on the Family and the Southern Baptist Convention. It has taken the uncharacteristic step of siding with the administration.

"We commend your steadfast preservation of federal policies that protect the freedom of religious organizations to consider religion in making employment decisions," it informed Obama last year. "Mr. President, your appreciation for the good that religious organizations contribute on a daily basis to our society is evident."

In this instance, Obama may be accused of ignoring the establishment clause of the First Amendment, which forbids government support of religion. But if so, it's because he has given too much deference to religious freedom rather than too little.

His commitment is also on display in defending churches against municipal governments that would prefer to do without them. Under federal law, houses of worship are assured equitable treatment in land-use decisions. But mayors and community groups often tell churches to go to the devil.

When that happens, they often find themselves at odds with the Civil Rights Division of the Justice Department. Last year, it forced the town of Schodack, N.Y., to retreat after it barred an evangelical church from renting space in a commercial area where nonreligious meetings were allowed.

It filed a brief in support of a Hasidic Jewish congregation's lawsuit against the city of Los Angeles, which had forbidden it to hold services in a private home. A federal court ordered the city to back off.

The administration has also intervened in cases where prisoners are denied religious literature. After a South Carolina sheriff prohibited inmates from getting devotional materials and other publications in the mail, the Justice Department sued. In the end, the county agreed to let inmates receive Bibles, Torahs, Qurans and related fare.

In doing all this, the administration isn't simply doing the politically appealing thing. Anything but. Those who endorse letting faith-based groups have a free hand in hiring are mostly religious conservatives who wouldn't vote for Obama if he resurrected the dead.

The congregations victimized by zoning regulations are too small to matter. Prison inmates generally can't vote. There is no detectable political gain in anything Obama is doing here.

University of Virginia law professor Douglas Laycock criticized the contraceptive mandate and opposed the administration in a Supreme Court case involving a teacher fired by a religious school. But he praises its efforts to help churches and prison inmates. And on the faith-based hiring issue, he says, Obama has actually been "kind of heroic."

The president's detractors may continue to portray him as a secular fanatic with, as Rick Santorum claims, an "overt hostility to faith in America." Before they do, though, they might want to remember the Ten Commandments—especially the one about bearing false witness.

Protecting Access to Birth Control Does Not Violate Religious Freedom

Robert Creamer

Robert Creamer is an author; a political organizer and strategist; a partner in Democracy Partners, a training organization for political organizers; and a senior strategist for Americans United for Change, a liberal policy group.

In many respects it is amazing that in 2012 there is a controversy over women's access to birth control.

Let's be clear, the current controversy over the [Barack] Obama administration's rules that require all employers who provide health insurance to provide birth control without a co-pay to its women employees, has nothing whatsoever to do with religious freedom.

It has everything to do with an attempt to take away women's access to easy, affordable birth control, no matter where they work.

Birth control is not controversial. Surveys show that 99 percent of women and 98 percent of Catholic women have used birth control at some time in their lives.

No one is trying to require that anyone else use birth control if it violates their religious convictions. But the convictions of some religious leaders should not be allowed to trump the rights of women employees to have access to birth control.

The Contraceptive Rule

The rule in question exempts 355,000 churches from this requirement since they presumably hire individuals who share the religious faith of the institutions in question. But it does not exempt universities and hospitals that may be owned by religious organizations, but serve—and employ—people of all faiths to engage in decidedly secular activities. These are not "religious institutions." They are engaged in the normal flow of commerce, even though they are owned by religious organizations.

The overwhelming majority of Americans oppose taking away the ability for women to have easy, affordable access to birth control.

Some religious leaders argue that they should not be required to pay for birth control coverage for their employees if they have religious objections to birth control. This argument ignores the fact that health insurance coverage is not a voluntary gift to employees. It is a part of their compensation package. If someone opposed the minimum wage on religious grounds—say because they believed it "discouraged individual initiative"—that wouldn't excuse them from having to pay the minimum wage.

If a Christian Science institution opposed invasive medical treatment on religious grounds, it would not be allowed to provide health care plans that fund only spiritual healing.

Many Americans opposed the Iraq War—some on religious grounds. That did not excuse them from paying taxes to the government.

Support for Contraception

The overwhelming majority of Americans oppose taking away the ability for women to have easy, affordable access to birth control. A Public Policy Polling survey released yesterday [February 7, 2012] found that 56 percent of voters support the decision to require health plans to cover prescription birth control with no additional out-of-pocket fees, while only 37 percent opposed. Fifty-three percent of Catholic voters favor the benefit.

Fifty-seven percent of voters think that women employed by Catholic hospitals and universities should have the same rights to contraceptive coverage as other women.

No doubt these numbers would be vastly higher if the poll were limited to the employees of those hospitals and universities because eliminating the requirement of coverage would cost the average woman $600 to $1,200 per year in out-of-pocket costs.

Twenty-eight states already require organizations that offer prescription insurance to cover contraception.

But ironically, requiring birth control coverage generally costs nothing to the institution that provides it. That's because by making birth control accessible, health plans cut down on the number of unwanted pregnancies that cost a great deal more. And of course they also cut down on the number of abortions.

That may help explain why many Catholic-owned universities already provide coverage for birth control. For instance, a Georgetown University spokesperson told *ThinkProgress* yesterday that employees "have access to health insurance plans offered and designed by national providers to a national pool. These plans include coverage for birth control."

The University of San Francisco, the University of Scranton, DePaul University in Chicago, Boston College—all have health insurance plans that cover contraception.

And, finally, this is nothing new. Twenty-eight states already require organizations that offer prescription insurance to cover contraception.

The Population Problem

Of course the shocking thing about this entire controversy is that there is a worldwide consensus that the use of birth control is one of society's most important moral priorities. Far from being something that should be discouraged, or is controversial, the use of birth control is critical to the survival and success of humanity.

In 1968, the world's population reached 3.5 billion people. On October 31, 2011, the *United Nations Population Division* reported that the world population had reached seven billion. It had *doubled* in 43 years.

It took 90,000 years of human development for the population to reach 1 billion. Over the last two centuries the population has grown by another six billion.

In fact, in the first 12 years of the 21st Century, we have already added a billion people to the planet.

It is simply not possible for this small planet to sustain that kind of exponential human population growth. If we do, the result will be poverty, war, the depletion of our natural resources and famine. Fundamentally, the Reverend Malthus was right—except that the result is not inevitable.

Population growth is not something that just happens to us. We can choose whether or not to reproduce and at what rates.

No force is required. The evidence shows that the population explosion stops where there is the availability of birth control and women have educational opportunity.

That's why it is our *moral imperative* to act responsibly and encourage each other to use birth control. And it's not a hard sell. Children are the greatest blessing you can have in life. But most people are eager to limit the number of children they have if they have access to contraception. We owe it to those children—to the next generation and the generation after that—to act responsibly and stabilize the size of the human population.

The moral thing to do is to make certain that every woman who wants it has access to birth control.

Catholic Bishops Want to Deny Women the Religious Freedom to Choose Contraception

Jessica Coblentz

Jessica Coblentz is a Catholic writer and a PhD student in theology at Boston College.

When the U.S. Conference of Catholic Bishops [USCCB] kicked off their "Fortnight for Freedom" campaign almost two weeks ago [June 21, 2012], they chose an auspicious feast day to start. On the Church's liturgical calendar, June 21 commemorates two martyrs who suffered political persecution: St. Thomas More and St. John Fisher, who were killed under Henry VIII for refusing to recognize him as the head of the Church of England. The American bishops have indicated they feel similarly besieged by political forces. To promote "our Christian and American heritage of liberty," they've organized two weeks of activism and prayer, culminating in a nationally televised liturgy on July 4, Independence Day—another date with clear significance for this U.S.-focused event.

At the forefront of the bishops' crusade is, of course, their opposition to the Obama administration's health insurance mandate requiring institutions—including many Catholic ones—to provide contraception coverage. Though the administration has tried to widen the mandate's exemptions, the USCCB argues that because Catholic doctrine does not condone contraception, the mandate constitutes a violation of religious liberty. The USCCB and its rallying cry have called the largest U.S. religious body, totaling more than 65 million members, into action. From Allentown, Pennsylvania, to Youngstown, Ohio, parishes and dioceses are hosting Fortnight for Freedom events, tolling church bells to "mark our gratitude for our First Freedom," praying the "Patriotic Rosary," and contacting Congress to voice their opposition to the mandate. The bishops are urging church members to text "FREEDOM" to join the campaign, and using church bulletin inserts to tell parishioners, "We cannot remain silent."

American Catholicism has a history of extolling the virtues of individual religious freedoms—even when it contradicts official Church teachings.

Denying Religious Freedom to Pro-Conception Catholic Women

Likewise, critics of the campaign refuse to remain silent. In the reaction against Fortnight for Freedom, some are responding to the bishops on their own terms. If the campaign is about religious liberty, they ask, then whose liberty is at stake? The bishops present the Catholic exercise of religious liberty as the ability to *reject* the use of contraception, or at least the financing of insurance plans that cover contraceptive services. The irony, to those on the other side, is that a campaign meant to promote religious liberty actually *denies* the religious freedom of many Catholic women, who rely on their personal religious convictions to determine their stance on contraception and the mandate. Studies show that as many as 98 percent of sexually experienced American Catholic women over the age of 18 have used contraception. A recent PRRI/RNS [Public Religion Research Institute/Religion News Service] poll reports that a majority of American Catholics do not see the contraception mandate as a threat to religious freedom, indicating that many hold a broader understanding of religious liberty than the bishops maintain. The debate surrounding the mandate, then, is not only about contraception and religious liberty. It is also about who gets to define religious liberty's very meaning.

Catholics for Choice (CFC), a reproductive rights group, has orchestrated the most expansive effort to actively engage the USCCB argument about religious liberty. In a statement, CFC asks the question, "Whose religious freedom are we talking about?" They argue, "No-cost contraception for the average woman, including many Catholic women, can mean following her religious beliefs, following her conscience." Likewise, parishioners at The Shrine of the Most Blessed Sacrament parish in Washington D.C. released a public statement criticizing the campaign's narrow depiction of religious liberty. "We, the faithful, are in danger of becoming pawns," they stated. "In no way do we feel that our religious freedom is at risk. We find it grotesque to have the call for this 'Fortnight' evoke the names of holy martyrs who died resisting tyranny." Other Catholics, from the editors of *Commonweal Magazine* to Bishop Stephen Blaire of Stockton, California, have criticized the shortsighted, partisan nature of the USCCB's charge that the mandate poses a threat to religious freedom.

So long as the all-male Catholic clergy solely possess the authority to identify what does and does not constitute a free, religiously-motivated choice worthy of legal protection, women have no official authority in Catholic religious liberty conversations whatsoever.

A Contentious Issue

Religious liberty has long been an important yet contentious issue for Catholics. The faith's status as a minority sect throughout much of American history set its members apart from other religious adherents and afforded a unique role in legal debates about religious freedom. Early court cases regarding Catholic parochial schools, for instance, were influential milestones in the development of church and state relations. But even as Catholics have long sought protection under religious liberty, they have not always been in agreement about it. Disagreement has often stemmed from the fact that American Catholicism has a history of extolling the virtues of individual religious freedoms—even when it contradicts official Church teachings.

In 1960, Jesuit John Courtney Murray—one of American Catholicism's most influential theologians on religious freedom—published his most famous book, *We Hold These Truths: Catholic Reflections on the American Proposition*, where he articulated the compatibility of Catholicism and American thought, particularly the First Amendment. Murray then went on to serve as a theological advisor during Vatican II, where he greatly influenced the Council's 1965 statement on religious freedom, *Dignitatis Humanae* (*DH*), which said an individual's conscience mediates "the imperatives of divine law." Consequently, one "is not to be forced to act in manner contrary to his conscience. Nor, on the other hand, is he to be restrained from acting in accordance with his conscience, especially in matters religious." The document assigned the responsibility of protecting religious liberty both to the state and to religious groups. Marking a turning point in Catholic teaching, it declared support for the constitutional protection of religious liberty—a stark contrast from the days of Christendom. The complementary limitations of church and state protected an individual's ability to act according to his or her conscience, especially concerning religious matters.

With the appearance of oral contraceptives in the early 1960s, little time passed before Catholics brought Vatican II's declarations on religious liberty to bear on contraception. In a memo to Boston's Richard Cardinal Cushing after Massachusetts decriminalized artificial contraception, John Courtney

Murray argued that contraception is a matter of private morality and thus one that ought to be protected by Catholics under religious liberty. When Pope Paul VI reaffirmed the Church's doctrinal stance against contraception in the 1968 papal letter *Humanae Vitae,* there was a public outcry from North American Catholics who opposed the letter on the grounds of religious liberty. In the United States, Catholic University's Charles Curran mobilized 600 theologians for a press conference where they announced their opposition to *Humanae Vitae,* arguing that dissent from the Vatican's position on contraception was permissible when discerned responsibly and for the sake of one's marriage. The Canadian Council of Catholic Bishops issued the Winnipeg Statement that year, asserting that any Catholic who "honestly chooses that course which seems right to him does so in good conscience," echoing the language of *Dignitatis Humanae.* Citing the "accepted principles of moral theology," the bishops argued that an act in good conscience is moral even if one acts against the Vatican's doctrinal teaching on contraception.

The Catholic theological tradition insists that religious liberty ought to protect the ability of a woman to obey her conscience.

Female Catholics' Choices and Religious Liberty

Critics of the bishops' current battle can call on this Catholic history of religious liberty and individual freedom. In their view, women's choices are an issue of religious liberty—not merely a threat to it. Still, who defines religious liberty remains a matter of authority—and a highly gendered one at that. When the USCCB conveys that the rejection of contraception is the only religiously-motivated choice that warrants the protection of religious liberty among Catholics, they assert the message that only church leaders have the authority to determine what counts as religious behavior. This strips other Catholics of the legitimate authority to negotiate their tradition when determining their own religiously-motivated actions. What is more, so long as the all-male Catholic clergy solely possess the authority to identify what does and does not constitute a free, religiously-motivated choice worthy of legal protection, women have no official authority in Catholic religious liberty conversations whatsoever. As it stands, the religious decisions and actions of all Catholics other than clergy—be they *for or against* contraception and contraceptive coverage—are seemingly insignificant in "Catholic" concerns about religious liberty.

The public rhetoric surrounding the HHS mandate has only reified the debates' gender lines. As [author] Michael Sean Winters observed earlier this year, the bishops are framing the mandate debate in terms of religious liberty in opposition to those who frame the discussion in terms of women's rights. A series of events in February bolstered the position of those advocating for a women's rights perspective—namely the absence of women at the official congressional hearing concerning the mandate and Rush Limbaugh's "slut" fiasco that arose in response to Sandra Fluke's testimony during an unofficial Democrat-sponsored hearing. The Fortnight for Freedom campaign can be viewed as an attempt to reemphasize the religious liberty stakes in the debate.

Yet the mandate is not simply a "women's issue" because it concerns contraception; the mandate is a "women's issue" because it concerns religious liberty, as the bishops insist, and the Catholic theological tradition insists that religious liberty ought to protect the ability of a woman to obey her conscience. The bishops, or anyone for that matter, need not theologically condone the contraceptive decisions of Catholic women in order to recognize them as exercises of free, religious choice. Yet the current rhetoric of the USCCB's "Fortnight for Freedom" campaign does not. With last week's Supreme Court decision to uphold the Affordable Care Act that contains the HHS contraception mandate, the USCCB has vowed to continue its opposition campaign. But if the bishops continue to exclude so many American Catholics from their representation of religious liberty—notably, the majority of Catholic Women—the USCCB fails in its own stated aim to protect the religious liberty of all.

CHAPTER 3

What Role Does Religion Play in International Politics?

Chapter Preface

Religion has long played a role in US foreign policy, but in 1998 the US Congress passed a law mandating that the president, the State Department, and the Congress promote religious liberty as a key part of US relations with other countries. The International Religious Freedom Act (IRFA) was signed into law by President Bill Clinton on October 27, 1998. Its overall goal is to convince other countries, including newly emerging democracies, that freedom of religion is a fundamental human right that must be honored in order to create national and global stability. The act gives the US president various options in responding to countries that commit or permit particularly egregious acts of religious persecution or violations of religious freedom. However, the IRFA also permits the president to waive sanctions against a particular country—an option that sometimes undermines the nation's commitment to religious freedom in favor of other national security priorities.

The IRFA came about because of congressional awareness of the growing pattern of religious persecution around the world. Many governments sanction one particular religion as the state religion and either openly tolerate religious persecution against minority faiths or take actions to restrict or otherwise interfere with the practices of other religions. Examples cited to support the legislation included Russia's religious restrictions; China's repression of Catholics and Protestant Christians, Buddhists in Tibet, and other religions; and Sudan's civil war, which was waged, in part, because of religious differences between ruling Muslims in the northern part of the country and Christians and other non-Muslims who mostly live in the south.

The IRFA obligates the Congress and the president to consider religious freedom issues when formulating US foreign policies. The president is required to identify specific countries that severely violate religious freedom—called countries of particular concern (CPC)—and then work with officials in the State Department and other foreign policy experts to respond to those countries. Title IV of the IFRA lists the options available in designing the US response. These include: a demarche (diplomatic message or protest); a public or private condemnation; cancellation, denial, or delay of cultural or scientific exchanges; cancellation, denial, or delay of state visits; withholding of humanitarian or other forms of US or international aid; and sanctions prohibiting the US government from entering into import or export agreements with the offending nation. Although the original legislation mandated sanctions against serious violators of religious freedom, the IFRA was amended before final passage to give the president the flexibility to refrain from taking punitive actions against a country shown to be violating religious freedom, in order to achieve other important US foreign policy or security interests.

The act sets up a structure for implementing its provisions, including the establishment of the Office of the International Religious Freedom at the US Department of State, which is led by an ambassador at large for international religious freedom. This office advises the president and the State Department on religious freedom issues and is responsible for publishing an annual report on international religious freedom (IRFR). This document describes the state of religious freedom existing in each country and explains what the United States is doing to respond to violators. The act also sets up a commission on international religious freedom (USCIRF) and a special advisor to the president on international religious freedom within the National Security Council. The commission is a body of experts, including the ambassador at large, that reviews annual reports and makes foreign policy recommendations to the president.

The passage of the IRFA made the United States unusual as one of the few countries in the world that promotes religious freedom openly as part of its foreign policy. Whether the act has achieved its goal of expanding religious freedom, however, is a matter of debate. Some observers note that the act has been helpful in publicizing the problem of religious persecution. The annual report on international religious freedom, in particular, is a resource used throughout the world to measure the degree to which religious freedom is being curtailed or threatened. However, critics argue that human rights, including religious freedom, continue to play only a small role in US foreign policy. They point out that the United States often grants waivers to countries known to be violators of religious freedom and in many other cases chooses weak sanctions against violators. Other critics assert that little has been done to advance the cause of religious freedom. For example, critics say the United States has failed to engage Islamic actors in Egypt, where the Arab Spring uprisings have produced an Islamist government. Still other critics argue that the United States has no right to push American ideas about religious freedom on other cultures that do not embrace this value. The authors of viewpoints included in this chapter address the basic question of whether religion is having an undue influence on international politics.

Religious Persecution Is Widespread Around the World

Andy Bannister

Andy Bannister is the Canadian director for Ravi Zacharias International Ministries (RZIM) Canada, a global team of speakers and writers who address issues related to faith, culture, politics, and society.

Dr. John Joseph was the Catholic Bishop of Faisalabad in Pakistan and a prominent human rights activist. On 6 May 1998, he travelled from his home to the city of Sahiwal to address a prayer meeting being held for victims of blasphemy cases. In Pakistan, the notorious 295-C law makes insulting Muhammad or the Qur'an [also called the Koran, the Islamic holy book] a crime punishable by death. The law is often used to falsely accuse religious minorities, especially Christians, and Dr. Joseph was concerned about one Christian in particular, Ayub Masih. Arrested in 1996 for allegedly violating the blasphemy laws, Ayub Masih had been held in solitary confinement in a tiny cell, denied medical care, and frequently abused. In April 1998, he had been formally found guilty and had been sentenced to death. After addressing the prayer meeting, Dr. Joseph made his way to the courthouse to the spot where, during the trial, somebody had shot at Ayub Masih and tried to assassinate him. At about 9:30 pm, Dr. Joseph took a pistol and took his own life. In a letter to a local newspaper, published after his death, he had written: "dedicated persons do not count the cost of the sacrifices they have to make".

Andy Bannister, "The Causes and Roots of Religious Persecution—Part 1," *The Bayview Review*, January 9, 2012. Copyright © 2012 by The Bayview Review. All rights reserved. Reproduced by permission.

Bishop John Joseph wanted to draw attention to the dire situation facing Pakistan's two million Christians. Everything else had been tried, but the international community seemed deaf to their plight. Frustrated, he concluded that only something so dramatic as his taking his own life would effect any change.

Sadly, it seems that his hope was misplaced. Although the international community is now more aware than ever of religious persecution, the situation is still bleak. It is presently estimated that some 200 million Christians in 60 countries live under daily threat of persecution. Between 2008 and 2009, 176,000 were killed. Some estimate that if nothing is done, then by 2025, an average of 210,000 Christians will be being killed each year.

Today, religious persecution occurs around the world in a wide variety of countries and contexts.

Just last week [January 2, 2012], the Catholic charity, Aid to the Church in Need, launched its annual report on religious freedom worldwide. It concluded that 75% of all religious persecution in the world is currently directed at Christian minorities. Archbishop Warda of Erbil in Iraq spoke about the difficulties in his country and commented:

We wonder if we will survive as a people in our own country. . . . The past is terrifying, the present is not promising.

Persecution is such a regular occurrence that it comes as no surprise that more than half the Christians in Iraq have fled. A community once numbering over a million is now down to about 150,000. Canon Andrew White who runs St. George's Anglican Church in Baghdad and is internationally known for his work on human rights and peace making, put it bluntly in an interview with CBS. Noting that the congregation at St. George's were mainly women and children the interviewer asked, "where are the men?" White replied: "They are mainly killed. Some are kidnapped. Some are killed. Here in this church, all of my original leadership were taken and killed."

How can it be, in the twenty-first century, that hundreds of millions of people are living in fear and are not free to worship or express their religious beliefs in safety?

Religious Persecution: A Global Tragedy

Religious persecution doesn't just effect Christians. In the last two millennia, some 200 million people have been killed because of their religious affiliation; those rates are not improving. Today, religious persecution occurs around the world in a wide variety of countries and contexts. One group who have also suffered tremendously are the Ahmadiyah Muslim sect. Considered heretical by mainstream Islam, the Ahmadiyah are banned and persecuted in many Muslim countries. For example, in Indonesia, the government passed a decree in 2008 requiring Ahmadiyah Muslims to "stop spreading interpretations and activities that deviate from the principal teachings of Islam". Those kind of signals from the government simply encourage extremist groups. Thus it was on 1 February 2011 that a mob of 1,500 men attacked twenty Ahmadiyah members in a village in Western Java. They broke into the house where the group was meeting, ordered the men to strip naked, then videoed them being beaten with sticks, hoes and machetes, before torching the building. Three died and six were wounded.

We could easily fill an entire library with such tragic stories. As Asma Jahangir, the UN Special Rapporteur on Religious Freedom or Belief wrote:

[Discrimination] based on religion or belief preventing individuals from fully enjoying all their human rights still occurs worldwide on a daily basis.

Where Is Persecution Happening?

All of this is deeply troubling. As with most human rights abuses, it's hard to discuss these things dispassionately: lives are broken, damaged and destroyed on a daily basis. But why is this happening? How can it be, in the twenty-first century, that hundreds of millions of people are living in fear and are not free to worship or express their religious beliefs in safety? Can we identify any patterns to religious persecution across the globe, any causes or trends that might help us formulate a response?

The answer to that question is yes. But let's begin by taking a step back and asking where precisely it is that religious persecution is happening. Whilst persecution is a global phenomena, there are patterns that we can track.

Brian Grim and Roger Finke, two sociologists who have produced some of the most recent analyses of religious persecution, have used a number of studies to answer this very question: where is persecution happening. Their figures look like this: [Muslim Majority 62%, Other Majority (Atheist, Buddhist, Hindu, Jewish) 85%, No Religion 33%, Christian Majority 28%, and World Average 43%.]

If we look at even higher rates of persecution, the differences are also striking:

Persecution of more than one thousand persons is present in 45 percent of Muslim-majority countries and 60 percent of the "Other Majority" religion countries, compared to 11 percent of Christian-majority countries and 8 percent of countries where no single religion holds a majority.

These figures are consistently backed up by other studies. For example, Open Doors, a well-respected Christian agency that lobbies on behalf of persecuted Christians, publishes an annual "World Watch List". Their 2011 report listed 51 countries of concern: 65% were Muslim-majority countries. Of the top ten human rights offenders, seven were Muslim-majority and two were communist atheistic states.

What could be the cause of these kind of figures? As Grim and Finke dig deeper and compare statistics from a wide range of countries, they quickly draw a conclusion. The common denominator, the common link—whether the country in which the persecution is occurring is Muslim or atheist, Hindu, Buddhist, or no-majority-religion—is religious regulation. There is a direct correlation between attempts by a state to control, regulate or restrict religious activity and religious persecution. Restriction on or regulation of religion is a surprisingly common phenomena. According to the Pew Forum:

[N]early 70 percent of the world's 6.8 billion people live in countries with high restrictions on religion, the brunt of which often falls on religious minorities.

Social pressures and state pressures on religious freedom often work together.

There are two ways that a state can attempt to control religious activity or restrict religious freedom within its borders. First, a government can use the full force of the state, for example by passing laws, arresting or harassing worshippers or religious leaders. So, for example, in China, the communist government has just marked the start of the Christian season of Lent by bulldozing churches and rounding up Christians, something it does every year, to remind them of the consequences of daring to be a religious believer in the officially atheistic People's Republic.

As well as using all the apparatus of the state, a government can also encourage or allow social pressure build up to make it hard for the members of a minority religious community to practice their faith. For example, in 2006 an Afghan man, Abdul Rahman, was arrested for apostasy [abandonment of religion]. The Afghan government, cognisant of the negative publicity the story was gaining as it spread around the world, were minded to release him. Senior Islamic clerics got wind of this and warned that they would incite people to kill him unless he reverted to Islam. When Abdul Rahman was released, three days later, hundreds of clerics and students marched in the streets crying "Death to Christians!"

Social pressures and state pressures on religious freedom often work together, mutually reinforcing one another. A tragic example of this occurred in Pakistan this year. On 4 January [2012], the governor of Punjab province, Salman Taseer, was getting into his car at a market when one of his own bodyguards opened fire and shot him 26 times. Why? The bodyguard was angry that Mr. Taseer was opposed to Pakistan's blasphemy law and had appealed for the pardon of a Christian woman, Asia Bibi, who had been sentenced to death for allegedly insulting Muhammad. A few months later, another politician, Shahbaz Bhatti, the Minority Affairs Minister and the only Christian in Pakistan's cabinet, was gunned down, again because of his well-publicised opposition to the blasphemy laws.

Those tragic stories illustrate the way that social pressures and government pressures on religious minorities work together and cause persecution. If the Pakistan government had the courage to remove the 295-C blasphemy law, this would remove much of the fuel from the fire that popular Islamist movements are trying to light.

How Do You Solve a Problem Like *Sharia*?

This connection between social restrictions, government restrictions and violent religious persecution also help to illuminate a phenomena we saw earlier: the extremely high rate of religious persecution in Muslim-majority countries. As

Brian Grim and Roger Finke put it:

> Religious persecution is not only more prevalent among Muslim-majority countries, but it also generally occurs at more severe levels.

The problem is simply this. Built into Islam is a ready-made system of religious law, *Sharia*. Because a whole codified body of religious law is readily available, governments in Muslim-majority countries face an ever present temptation to draw upon or incorporate aspects of *Sharia* into their legal systems. Unlike many Western bodies of law, *Sharia* is far more wide-ranging and includes regulations that encompass morality and religion and many of its stipulations have implications for religious minorities.

Many Muslim countries have incorporated *Sharia* law, or aspects of it into their legal system and constitutions. Those that haven't face a growing popular pressure to do so. A 2006 Gallup survey of ten Muslim-majority countries found that 79% wanted *Sharia* in some form. Indeed, 66% of Egyptians and 60% of Pakistanis said they wanted *Sharia* as the only source of legislation. Even an astonishing 40% of British Muslims said they wanted *Sharia*.

When it comes to religious persecution, it is vital to stress that the problem is not Muslims. The problem is Sharia.

The implementation of *Sharia* law is directly connected to the problems of religious freedom and religious persecution in Muslim-majority countries, the states where persecution rates are among the highest in the world. But here we enter a very difficult area of discussion. When it comes to talking about Islam and these kind of issues, there are two traps one can fall into. One is to be overly critical, lumping all Muslims together as a group, not appreciating the wide diversity and ranges of opinion within the world's 1.6 billion Muslims. But if being overly critical is one error, the other is to be overly timid and to not ask any difficult questions or to raise any controversial issues.

How can we best navigate between these two pitfalls? I have been researching, teaching and writing on Islam for fifteen years now and do so unapologetically as a Christian. For me, I've found an observation made by Anglican vicar and human rights activist, Mark Durie, very helpful. Mark speaks of the need to hold two things together—love and respect for the other but also truth. He writes:

> Love for the other and truth are two attributes to be held together, the one complementing the other. Truth without love can be harsh and even cruel, but love without truth can be equally as dangerous as, lacking discernment, it steers the soul into shipwreck after shipwreck.

We also need to be willing to recognise something that's often neglected in these discussions. The importance of different worldviews. Just as different political ideologies can produce vastly different societies, even next door to one another—compare communist North with capitalist South Korea—so different religious worldviews exert very different influences. The Qur'an does not produce the same kinds of societies as the Judeo-Christian worldview whilst Buddhist, Hinduism or Marxist-Atheism produce different results again.

But when it comes to religious persecution, it is vital to stress that the problem is not *Muslims*. The problem is *Sharia*. To misquote Rogers and Hammerstein: how do you solve a problem like *Sharia*?

Islam Has Emerged as a Political Force in the Middle East

Michael A. Lange

Michael A. Lange is head of the political dialogue and analysis team at the Department for European and International Cooperation of Konrad-Adenauer-Stiftung, a political party foundation in Berlin, Germany.

Following the election of the Ennahda Party in Tunisia in October 2011 and the Justice and Development Party (PJD) in Morocco in November 2011, the decisive victory by the Muslim Brotherhood's Freedom and Justice Party (FJP) in the parliamentary elections in Egypt at the turn of the year 2011/2012 seemed to confirm an Islamic trend: the Arab Spring has since led to a conspicuous "Islamic awakening".

A Continuing Islamic Trend

Forthcoming elections in Algeria and Libya, as well as planned elections in Yemen and the Palestinian Autonomous Area are already looming. There is much evidence to suggest that this Islamic trend will continue. Without free elections by secret ballot, it is not possible to install those requisite democratically legitimate constitutional bodies that are called upon to exert a determining influence on the future political order of their countries. All elections, whether they are for short-term constituent assemblies or for representative bodies elected for full legislative periods, will have a decisive influence not only on the soon to be relevant party political spectrum, but also on the political balance of power in the various Arab states that are currently undergoing comprehensive political transformation.

Egypt, the Arab country with the largest population and therefore traditionally the most influential, will have a particularly important role to play in this regional transition process. If political transition is successful in Egypt, then it is possible that the process of democratic change in the Arab world will continue and conceivably prevail. If transition is seen to fail there early on, then it will also be more difficult for other countries in the region to bring their own transition processes to a successful conclusion. Egypt, which has a comparatively heterogeneous population, will be a decisive test case, not only for the future relationship between Islam-inspired and secular political movements, but also for relations between ultra-orthodox and liberal forms of Islam. Additionally, the expected re-positioning of the Egyptian military within a new constitutional system will be a significant challenge in itself, and it will no doubt have an influence on similar security sector reform processes in neighbouring Arab countries.

[The] sum of imponderables will not only continue to encumber the transition process in Egypt, but also preoccupy the entire region for a long time to come.

What are the likely ramifications for politics, the economy and society of policies that will influence the government's future work, if the policies are more clearly oriented towards the implementation of Islamic Sharia law? What rights and how much tolerance will religious and secular minorities receive in a new political order of this kind, without inciting a cultural war? How will the new Islamic parties create the kind of economic new beginning that is needed without coming into conflict with the restrictive tenets of Islam, and what stance should European countries, especially Germany, take towards these election victors with their Islamic leanings? Will future political dialogue with governments determined by Islamic powers in North African countries that are undergoing transition continue to be characterized by the kind of scepticism EU [European Union] countries displayed in reaction to the 2006 election victory of Hamas (basically another offshoot of the Muslim Brotherhood, who were victorious in Egypt), or will the practicalities of *Realpolitik* call for a re-evaluation? All these questions need to be considered when viewing the political upheavals that will be related to significant electoral victories for political Islam in North Africa.

Transition Concepts: Road Maps for Change

The demands of the "rebellious youth" in Tunisia and Egypt, as well as other autocratic states such as Libya and Syria, for more human rights and social justice, as part of a comprehensive restructuring of the existing political order, won the almost wholehearted support of political observers in Europe from the onset. However, in recent months these demands have taken the various countries down some very different paths. Since the power structures that were firmly established only a few months ago have not yet demonstrated the necessary willingness to introduce the kind of reforms that are needed to lead their countries out of the political cul-de-sac of unresolved succession issues and unsatisfactory political and economic reform processes, a different kind of change to the political order has been set in motion, which will undoubtedly be even more challenging, in as much as the potential political ramifications of such a change are far more difficult to assess. It is important not only to structure these changes in a coherent manner, but to do so in as peaceful a way as possible, so that the changes lead to an outcome that is acceptable to all concerned. This has been and continues to be no easy task.

The individual countries in North Africa have since chosen entirely different paths on the way to a new political order. The transition processes in the various countries differ not only in terms of protagonists, but also in terms of the intensity of the accompanying resistance and protests. Following the removal or expulsion of their former autocratic leaders, each of the countries initially had to deal with the issue of what to do with the "remains of the ruling political class", who had close ties to former autocratic regimes. This sum of imponderables will not only continue to encumber the transition process in Egypt, but also preoccupy the entire region for a long time to come. It will certainly be some time before the people of these countries are able to return to their familiar, not particularly political, everyday lives. Awaiting subsidence of the current tumultuous political situation will require much patience from the citizens of these countries. There are many good reasons for Europe in particular to hope that they will find this patience. If they do not, it seems unlikely that the current transition process will be brought to a successful conclusion, with all the attendant unpleasant consequences for political dialogue and economic cooperation with the countries of North Africa.

Fear the Muslim Brotherhood

Andrew C. McCarthy

Andrew C. McCarthy is an author and a senior fellow at the National Review Institute, a conservative public policy and advocacy organization.

At the *Daily Beast*, Bruce Riedel has posted an essay called "Don't fear Egypt's Muslim Brotherhood," the classic, conventional-wisdom response to the crisis in Egypt. The Muslim Brotherhood is just fine, he'd have you believe, no need to worry. After all, the Brothers have even renounced violence!

One might wonder how an organization can be thought to have renounced violence when it has inspired more jihadists than any other, and when its Palestinian branch, the Islamic Resistance Movement, is probably more familiar to you by the name Hamas—a terrorist organization committed by charter to the violent destruction of Israel. Indeed, in recent years, the Brotherhood (a.k.a., the Ikhwan) has enthusiastically praised jihad and even applauded—albeit in more muted tones— Osama bin Laden. None of that, though, is an obstacle for Mr. Riedel, a former CIA officer who is now a Brookings scholar and Obama administration national-security adviser. Following the template the progressive (and bipartisan) foreign-policy establishment has been sculpting for years, his "no worries" conclusion is woven from a laughably incomplete history of the Ikhwan.

By his account, Brotherhood founder Hassan al-Banna "preached a fundamentalist Islamism and advocated the creation of an Islamic Egypt, but he was also open to importing techniques of political organization and propaganda from Eu-

Andrew C. McCarthy, "Fear the Muslim Brotherhood," *National Review Online*, January 31, 2011. Copyright © 2011 by National Review Online. All rights reserved. Reproduced by permission.

rope that rapidly made the Brotherhood a fixture in Egyptian politics." What this omits, as I recount in *The Grand Jihad*, is that terrorism and paramilitary training were core parts of Banna's program. It is by leveraging the resulting atmosphere of intimidation that the Brotherhood's "politics" have achieved success. The Ikhwan's activist organizations follow the same program in the United States, where they enjoy outsize political influence because of the terrorist onslaught.

Banna was a practical revolutionary. On the one hand, he instructed his votaries to prepare for violence. They had to understand that, in the end—when the time was right, when the Brotherhood was finally strong enough that violent attacks would more likely achieve Ikhwan objectives than provoke crippling blowback—violence would surely be necessary to complete the revolution (meaning, to institute sharia, Islam's legal-political framework). Meanwhile, on the other hand, he taught that the Brothers should take whatever they could get from the regime, the political system, the legal system, and the culture. He shrewdly realized that, if the Brothers did not overplay their hand, if they duped the media, the intelligentsia, and the public into seeing them as fighters for social justice, these institutions would be apt to make substantial concessions. Appeasement, he knew, is often a society's first response to a threat it does not wish to believe is existential.

Here's Riedel again:

> By World War 2, [the Brotherhood] became more violent in its opposition to the British and the British-dominated monarchy, sponsoring assassinations and mass violence. After the army seized power in 1952, [the Brotherhood] briefly flirted with supporting Gamal Abdel Nasser's government but then moved into opposition. Nasser ruthlessly suppressed it.

This history is selective to the point of parody. The Brotherhood did not suddenly become violent (or "more violent") during World War II. It was violent from its origins two decades earlier. This fact—along with Egyptian Islamic society's deep antipathy toward the West and its attraction to the Nazis' virulent anti-Semitism—is what gradually beat European powers, especially Britain, into withdrawal.

Banna himself was killed in 1949, during the Brotherhood's revolt against the British-backed monarchy. Thereafter, the Brotherhood did not wait until after the Free Officers Movement seized power to flirt with Nasser. They were part of the coup, Nasser having personally lobbied Sayyid Qutb (the most significant Ikhwan figure after Banna's death) for an alliance.

Omitting this detail helps Riedel whitewash the Brothers' complicity in what befell them. The Ikhwan did not seamlessly "move into the opposition" once Nasser came to power. First, it deemed itself double-crossed by Nasser, who had wooed the Brotherhood into the coup by signaling sympathy for its Islamist agenda but then, once in power, declined to implement elements of sharia. Furthermore, Nasser did not just wake up one day and begin "ruthlessly suppressing" the Brotherhood; the Ikhwan tried to assassinate him. It was at that point, when the Islamist coup attempt against the new regime failed, that the strongman cracked down relentlessly.

Riedel next asserts: "Nasser and his successors, Anwar Sadat and Mubarak, have alternatively repressed and demonized the Brotherhood or tolerated it as an anti-communist and right-wing opposition." This, too, is hopelessly wrong and incomplete. To begin with, regardless of how obdurately progressives repeat the claim, Islamism is not a right-wing movement. The Brotherhood's is a revolutionary program, the political and economic components of which are essentially socialist. It is no accident that Islamists in America are among the staunchest supporters of Obamacare and other redistributionist elements of the Obama agenda. In his *Social Justice in Islam*, Qutb concludes that Marx's system is far superior to capitalism, which Islamists deplore. Communism, he argues, faltered principally in its rigid economic determinism, thus missing the spiritual components of Allah's totalitarian plan—

though Qutb compared it favorably to Christianity, which he saw as insufficiently attentive to earthly concerns.

Nasser's persecution of the Ikhwan led many of its leading figures to flee Egypt for Saudi Arabia, where the Brothers were welcomed because they were perceived, quite correctly, as urbane but stalwart jihadists who would greatly benefit a backwards society—especially its education system (Banna and Qutb were both academics, and the Brotherhood teemed with professionals trained in many disciplines). The toxic mix of Saudi billions and Brotherhood ideology—the marriage of Saudi Wahhabism and Brotherhood Salafism—created the modern Islamist movement and inspired many of the terrorist organizations (including al-Qaeda) and other Islamist agitators by which we are confronted today. That Wahhabism and Salafism are fundamentalist doctrines does not make them right-wing. In fact, Islamism is in a virulent historical phase, and is a far more daunting challenge to the West than it was a half-century ago, precisely because its lavishly funded extremism has overwhelmed the conservative constraints of Arab culture.

The Brotherhood seems comparatively moderate, if only because the most horrific atrocities have been committed by two even worse terrorist organizations.

Sadat pivoted away from his predecessor's immersion of Egypt into the Soviet orbit. He did indeed invite the Ikhwan to return home, as Riedel indicates. Sadat knew the Brothers were bad news, but—much like today's geopolitical big thinkers—he hubristically believed he could control the damage, betting that the Ikhwan would be more a thorn in the side of the jilted Nasserite Communists than a nuisance for the successor regime. Riedel's readers may not appreciate what a naïve wager that was, since he fails to mention that the Brotherhood eventually murdered Sadat in a 1981 coup attempt—in accordance with a fatwa issued by Sheikh Omar Abdel Rahman (later of World Trade Center-bombing fame) after Sadat made peace with the hated "Zionist entity."

Sadat's successor, Mubarak, is undeniably a tyrant who has kept emergency powers in force through the three decades since Sadat's assassination. Any fair assessment, however, must concede that he has had his reasons. Egypt is not just plagued by economic stagnation and inequality; it has been brutalized by jihadist terror. It would be fair enough—though by no means completely convincing—for Riedel and others to argue that Mubarak's reign has been overkill. It makes no sense, though, to ignore both the reason emergency powers were instituted in the first place and the myriad excuses jihadists have given Mubarak to maintain them.

On that score, the Brotherhood seems comparatively moderate, if only because the most horrific atrocities have been committed by two even worse terrorist organizations—Abdel Rahman's Gamaat al Islamia and Ayman al-Zawahiri's Islamic Jihad, both precursors to al-Qaeda (in which Zawahiri is bin Laden's deputy). Of course, Zawahiri—like bin Laden and such al-Qaeda chieftains as 9/11 architect Khalid Sheikh Mohammed—came of age as a Muslim Brother, and Abdel Rahman notoriously had a close working relationship with the Ikhwan. But even if we close our eyes to the Ikhwan's contributions to terrorist violence in Egypt since its attempted forcible overthrow of the regime in 1981, we must not overlook the sophisticated game the Ikhwan plays when it comes to terrorism.

Occasionally, the Brotherhood condemns terrorist attacks, but not because it regards terrorist violence as wrong per se. Instead, attacks are criticized either as situationally condemnable (al-Qaeda's 1998 embassy bombings, though directed at American interests, killed many Muslims and were not supported by an authoritative fatwa), or as counterproductive (the 9/11 attacks provoked a backlash that resulted in the invasion and occupation of Muslim countries, the killing of many Muslims, and severe setbacks to the cause of spreading Islam). Yet, on other occasions, particularly in the Arab press, the Ikhwan embraces violence—fueling Hamas and endorsing the murder of Americans in Iraq.

Our see-no-Islamic-evil foreign-policy establishment blathers on about the Brotherhood's purported renunciation of violence.

In addition, the Brotherhood even continues to lionize Osama bin Laden. In 2008, for example, "Supreme Guide" Muhammad Mahdi Akef lauded al-Qaeda's emir, saying that bin Laden is not a terrorist at all but a "mujahid," a term of honor for a jihad warrior. The Supreme Guide had "no doubt" about bin Laden's "sincerity in resisting the occupation," a point on which he proclaimed bin Laden "close to Allah on high." Yes, Akef said, the Brotherhood opposed the killing of "civilians"—and note that, in Brotherhood ideology, one who assists "occupiers" or is deemed to oppose Islam is not a civilian. But Akef affirmed the Brotherhood's support for al-Qaeda's "activities against the occupiers."

By this point, the Ikhwan's terror cheerleading should surprise no one—no more than we should be surprised when the Brotherhood's sharia compass, Sheikh Yusuf Qaradawi, approves suicide bombings or unleashes rioting over mere cartoons; no more than when the Ikhwan's Hamas faction reaffirms its foundational pledge to destroy Israel. Still, just in case it is not obvious enough that the "Brotherhood renounces violence" canard is just that, a canard, consider Akef's explicit call for jihad in Egypt just two years ago, saying that the time "requires the raising of the young people on the basis of the principles of jihad so as to create mujahideen [there's that word again] who love to die as much as others love to live, and who can perform their duty towards their God, themselves, and their homeland." That leitmotif—*We love death more than you love life*—has been a staple of every jihadist from bin Laden through Maj. Nidal Hasan, the Fort Hood killer.

To this day, the Brotherhood's motto remains, "Allah is our objective, the Prophet is our leader, the Koran is our law, Jihad is our way, and dying in the way of Allah is our highest hope. Allahu akbar!" Still, our see-no-Islamic-evil foreign-policy establishment blathers on about the Brotherhood's purported renunciation of violence—and never you mind that, with or without violence, its commitment is, as Qaradawi puts it, to "conquer America" and "conquer Europe." It is necessary to whitewash the Ikhwan's brutal legacy and its tyrannical designs in order to fit it into the experts' paradigm: history for simpletons. This substitute for thinking holds that, as Secretary of State Condoleezza Rice famously told an Egyptian audience in 2005, America has too often opted for stability rather than freedom. As a result, the story goes, our nation has chosen to support dictators when we should have been supporting . . . never mind that.

The Obama administration has courted Egyptian Islamists from the start.

But we have to mind that. History is rarely a Manichean contest between good and evil. It's not a choice between the pro-Western shah and Iranian freedom, but between the shah and Khomeini's ruthless Islamist revolution. It's not a choice between the pro-Western Musharraf and Pakistani freedom, but between Musharraf and a tense alliance of kleptocratic socialists and Islamists. Back in the 1940s, it was not a choice between the British-backed monarchy and Egyptian freedom, but between the monarchy and a conglomeration of Nasserite pan-Arab socialists, Soviet Communists, and Brotherhood Islamists. And today, the choice is not between the pro-

American Mubarak and Egyptian freedom; it is a question of whether to offer tepid support to a pro-American dictator or encourage swift transition to a different kind of tyranny—one certain to be a lot worse for us, for the West at large, and for our Israeli ally: the Muslim Brotherhood tempered only, if at all, by Mohamed ElBaradei, an anti-American leftist who willfully abetted Iran's nuclear ambitions while running the International Atomic Energy Agency.

History is not a quest for freedom. This is particularly true in the Islamic ummah, where the concept of freedom is not reasoned self-determination, as in the West, but nearly the opposite: perfect submission to Allah's representative on earth, the Islamic state. Coupled with a Western myopia that elevates democratic forms over the culture of liberty, the failure to heed this truth has, in just the past few years, put Hamas in charge of Gaza, positioned Hezbollah to topple the Lebanese government, and presented Islamists with Kosovo—an enduring sign that, where Islam is concerned, the West can be counted on to back away even from the fundamental principle that a sovereign nation's territorial integrity is inviolable.

The Obama administration has courted Egyptian Islamists from the start. It invited the Muslim Brotherhood to the president's 2009 Cairo speech, even though the organization is officially banned in Egypt. It has rolled out the red carpet to the Brotherhood's Islamist infrastructure in the U.S.—CAIR, the Muslim American Society, the Islamic Society of North America, the Ground Zero mosque activists—even though many of them have a documented history of Hamas support. To be sure, the current administration has not been singular in this regard. The courting of Ikhwan-allied Islamists has been a bipartisan project since the early 1990s, and elements of the intelligence community and the State Department have long agitated for a license to cultivate the Brotherhood overtly. They think what Anwar Sadat thought: Hey, we can work with these guys.

There is a very good chance we are about to reap what they've sown. We ought to be very afraid.

Forget the Brotherhood. It's Egypt's Generals Who Should Worry Us

Mehdi Hasan

Mehdi Hasan is a contributing writer for the New Statesman, *a British magazine that focuses on current affairs, world politics, and the arts.*

Should we be worried by the Muslim Brotherhood's victory in the Egyptian presidential election? Earlier this year, I interviewed Wael Ghonim, the young Google executive and anti-Mubarak activist who became the face of Egypt's inspiring revolution back in January and February of 2011.

Was he concerned by the Muslim Brotherhood's victory in Egypt's parliamentary elections in December? "No," he said. "The western media, and even some sections of the Arab media, are taking a very pessimistic view. But what is going on here is very healthy. The Muslim Brotherhood was the strongest party and got almost 50 per cent of the seats." He argued: "We should give democracy a chance and respect the choices of the Egyptian people."

Six months on, Ghonim remains hopeful. "1st elected civilian in modern history of Egypt as President," he tweeted, after the Muslim Brotherhood's Mohammed Morsi's cliffhanger victory over the Mubarak loyalist and ex-premier Ahmed Shafiq in the presidential run-off on 24 June. "Critical milestone. Revolution isn't an event, it's a process so it continues!"

There is a stark contrast between the undimmed optimism of Ghonim—the young, secular, liberal Egyptian activist—and the pessimism of western politicians and pundits, petrified by the rise of the dastardly Muslim Brotherhood. The latter, the world's oldest and most influential Islamist movement, is seen by many as a threat to women's rights, non-Muslims and, of course, western interests in the Middle East.

Bigger Picture

We need to take a collective step back and look again at the big picture. The Arab world's most populous nation has, for the first time, elected its own head of state in a multi-candidate, free and fair election. The repulsive Hosni Mubarak and his corrupt sons are gone; their 30-year reign of terror is over. Lest we forget, in 2006, Morsi was in prison and Mubarak was in the presidential palace; today, just six years later, Mubarak is in prison and Morsi is in the palace. This is a remarkable and historic moment for Egypt, and for the wider Arab world.

The changes we want to see in the Middle East won't happen overnight. Revolutions . . . take time.

That said, Morsi is far from perfect. He wasn't even the Muslim Brotherhood's first choice as presidential candidate (the party's deputy chairman, Khairat al-Shater, was barred from standing). Morsi is a 9/11 conspiracy theorist ("Something must have happened from the inside," he declared in May 2010) who has said that the state should enforce sharia law and has called for women and Christians to be banned from running for president.

But we shouldn't write him off—yet. On winning the election, he promptly quit the Brotherhood, pledged to be the "president of all Egyptians" and promised to appoint a cabinet of "technocrats", not card-carrying Islamists.

Here in the west, however, our obsession with Muslim Brothers such as Morsi distracts attention from two points.

First, the changes we want to see in the Middle East won't happen overnight. Revolutions, as Ghonim pointed out, take time. Yet there seems to be a willful amnesia on the part of some pessimistic pundits in the west.

At a recent Oxford Union debate on the future of the Arab spring, a retired US general, Keith Dayton, decried the ongoing discrimination against women, homosexuals and religious minorities in countries such as Egypt and Libya. I couldn't help but point out to the good general that it took his own country, "the land of the free", 89 years, between independence in 1776 and the passage of the Thirteenth Amendment in 1865, to abolish slavery. Here in the UK, there was a 96-year gap between the first Reform Act of 1832, which extended the franchise to property owners, and the sixth Reform Act of 1928, which gave women the vote on the same terms as men.

Shamefully, the United States has spent the past three decades propping up Egypt's generals.

Second, the most powerful man in Egypt is not President-Elect Morsi but Field Marshal Hussein Tantawi, the chairman of the Supreme Council of the Armed Forces (SCAF), which, in effect, has ruled Egypt since Mubarak left office on 11 February 2011.

It is the military that dominates modern Egyptian politics. All four presidents since a group of officers overthrew the monarchy in 1952 have come from the military. The country's armed forces—the world's tenth-biggest—are believed to control between 30 and 40 per cent of the Egyptian economy. And in June SCAF dissolved the elected parliament and claimed legislative power for itself. Egypt, in the words of one commentator, is a military with a state rather than a state with a military.

Making Waives

Shamefully, the United States has spent the past three decades propping up Egypt's generals. Since the 1979 Egypt-Israel peace treaty, the US has lavished $35bn in aid on the Egyptian military, making it the largest recipient of US military and economic aid after Israel.

But things have changed since the fall of Mubarak, right? Wrong. "Once imperilled, US aid to Egypt is restored", read the headline in the *New York Times* on 23 March. In December 2011, President Obama signed a law that required the Egyptian government to support the transition to civilian government and protect freedoms of speech and assembly before any US military aid could be approved. But, said the *NYT*, Secretary of State Hillary Clinton "used her authority under the new law to waive a requirement that she certify Egypt's protection of human rights", thereby allowing "the Egyptian military to continue to arm and equip its forces". So much for Obama's vow, in May 2011, "to promote reform across the region, and to support transitions to democracy".

The biggest obstacles to greater freedom and democracy in Egypt are the generals, not the Brothers. Yet they, too, like their former boss Mubarak, as well as their paymasters in the US, are on the wrong side of history. The "reform genie", as an unnamed western diplomat told the *Financial Times* on 20 June, is out of the bottle. The Egyptian people, whether secularist or Islamist, Muslim or Christian, won't tolerate another three decades of Mubarak-style rule. As Ghonim told his half-million followers on Twitter in June: "The only thing that will make us go back to living in fear, oppression and silence is a time machine—they haven't invented that yet."

Egyptians Rethink Religion and Politics as They Vote

Lucy Chumbley

Lucy Chumbley is a journalist based in Washington, DC.

As Egyptians vote to elect their next president, what are they looking for? While Western media focus on the role of religious parties and worry about unrest, a University of Maryland poll released on May 21 at the Brookings Institution shows Egyptians are looking toward a more nuanced model for religion and politics—and that there are reasons to be optimistic about Egypt's political transition.

Introducing the findings of the 2012 Public Opinion Survey in Egypt, conducted May 4–10 ahead of the Egyptian presidential debate, principal investigator Shibley Telhami, Senior Fellow at Brookings and the Anwar Sadat Professor for Peace and Development at the University of Maryland, identified presidential candidates Abdel Moneim Aboul Fotouh, formerly affiliated with the Muslim Brotherhood, and Amr Moussa, Egypt's former Minister of Foreign Affairs and Secretary-General of the Arab League, as frontrunners.

The top criteria Egyptians identified as being important in their next president were personal trust in the candidates and their position on the economy, with the role of religion in politics and party affiliation at the bottom of the list.

Though religion was not a deciding factor in the choice of candidates, Telhami said, 66 percent of those questioned favored using shariah as the basis of Egyptian law. But of that number, just 17 percent said it should be interpreted literally, with 83 percent advocating adapting it to contemporary times.

"Shariah is very important psychologically for most Muslims, but the way they interpret it is flexible", Telhami said. Although religion remains important for Egyptians, the role it will take when it comes to the legal system is yet unknown. The fact that Egyptians do not see Islamic principles as monolithic or immutable is a point that those observing the country would do well to remember as the country transitions.

The Egyptian people are looking at their political system holistically, evidenced by the fact that they are differentiating between the president and Parliament.

When asked about what role religion should play in the political system, 54 percent of respondents identified Turkey as the model which most closely matched their aspirations from the choices offered: Iran, Turkey, Tunisia, Malaysia and Morocco. Turkey also emerged as a leading influence in other areas: Outside Egypt, 63 percent of respondents identified Turkish Prime Minister Recep Tayyip Erdogan as the leader they most admired in an open question, while in a question that did not exclude Egyptian leaders, Erdogan came third after former Egyptian presidents Anwar Sadat and Gamal Abdel Nasser.

In a world where there could be just one superpower (Egypt excluded), 41 percent of those polled said they would like to see Turkey in that place.

"The Turkish model clearly is the one that resonates most so far with Egyptians," Telhami said.

Beyond the role of religion and politics, the poll indicates that the Egyptian people are looking at their political system holistically, evidenced by the fact that they are differentiating between the president and Parliament, he added.

While Egyptians listed personal trust, the economy, and track record and experience as being most important in determining how they will vote in the presidential elections, the key factors determining their choices in the parliamentary elections were different. Here, the political party was seen as most important, followed by record, experience and the economy.

Noting that the poll's results are indicative of trends rather than election results due to the lack of benchmarking data, Telhami pointed out that these findings for the most part track the conventional wisdom in Egypt, though the political situation continues to be "fluid."

Most Egyptians he consulted "were not surprised by the results," he said: "It matched the general perception."

Conducted using a nationally representative stratified sample of 773 people from cities and rural areas, the poll was carried out via professional face-to-face interviews.

"Most political parties are really behind peaceful mobilization," Telhami said, noting that Egypt—a country of 80 million—has come a long way in the last year and a half. "That's pretty optimistic stuff, I think."

Good Government Does Not Have to Be Secular

Elizabeth Shakman Hurd

Elizabeth Shakman Hurd is an assistant professor of political science at Northwestern University in Evanston, Illinois. She speaks and writes frequently on Middle East politics and religion issues and is the author of The Politics of Secularism in International Relations *(2007).*

It is striking the extent to which the word "secular"—and related terms such as secular democracy and secular leaders—are relatively synonymous with all that is good, right and universal in many Western accounts of developments in Egypt.

The indiscriminate association of the secular with good governance and the natural domain of rational self-interest and universalist ethics contrasts with the idea of Islam as irrational and decidedly not secular.

But as history plays out so dramatically in the Middle East, it is time to replace such simplistic views of Muslim-majority societies with a much more complicated story about religion and politics in Egypt.

A History of Repressions

The Muslim Brotherhood, founded in 1928 and still officially outlawed in Egypt, is anxiously depicted in these accounts as "Islamist" and represented as a potential danger that might result from the emergence of democracy in Egypt. Political positions expressed through reference to Islamic tradition, history, or politics are assimilated into the category of "bad" politics and assumed to threaten normal, rational, and democratic politics. Political Islam is seen as a throwback to pre-modern forms of Muslim political order.

Washington remained silent as the Mubarak regime arrested hundreds of Brothers and transferred dozens to military courts.

Thus, aligning Western interests with a secular dictator has been seen as preferable to encouraging democratic measures that would accommodate the interests of so-called unreliable and dangerous Islamists.

The United States has stood forcefully and famously behind this state-instituted and highly securitized secular-religious oppositional binary as a means of defending its interests in the region. These are defined primarily as ensuring Israeli security, pursuing the war on terror, and guaranteeing access to oil.

After Egypt's 2005 parliamentary elections, in which the Muslim Brotherhood gained one-fifth of the seats in parliament, U.S. pressure on the [Hosni] Mubarak regime decreased and then ceased entirely after Hamas' victory in 2006. Washington remained silent as the Mubarak regime arrested hundreds of Brothers and transferred dozens to military courts.

No Reason to Fear Islamic Government

But today the Egyptian people and a powerful anti-Mubarak coalition are overturning this entire structure of domination, upheld by Mubarak and aided and abetted by the Americans and the Europeans for decades. The future is up for grabs.

Misguided Western constructs of Islamist politics have empowered Mubarak and other autocrats throughout the region. Such thinking fails to address the realities of contemporary politics in states in which these movements have gained a strong and legitimate political foothold. These cannot be washed away by wishful thinking in Washington, London, or Jerusalem.

Such a hostile attitude toward the Muslim Brotherhood also is unfounded. According to Nathan Brown, "a lot of their program is just standard reform stuff—independence of the judiciary, the end of corruption, protecting the environment. Especially when they got more political over the last 10 years or so, what they really began to push was a very general reform language that takes Islamic coloration in some areas. But an awful lot of it is consistent with other reform programs coming from reformists all over the political spectrum."

It remains to be seen whether Western decision-makers and pundits will display the political courage and intellectual creativity needed to move beyond the false choice between secular dictators and "crazy Islamists" and support real democracy in the Middle East, for a change. The opposite of democratic is not Islamic. It is military dictatorship.

CHAPTER 4

How Should the United States Balance Religion and Politics in the Future?

Chapter Preface

Although the First Amendment's guarantee of freedom of religion and separation of church and state have been part of American law for more than two centuries, there is still debate in America about how religion should be balanced with secular government interests. Historically, the US Supreme Court has closely scrutinized any government action that infringes on First Amendment rights, including freedom of religion. However, the Supreme Court decisions on religion in the 1980s shifted towards allowing the government to restrict religious freedom as long as the government action treated all religions the same way. This trend upset many religious organizations and civil rights groups, and led to the passage in 1993 of the Religious Freedom Restoration Act (RFRA)—legislation that required governments to have a compelling state interest before limiting freedom of religion. This law basically reinstated the earlier Supreme Court approach of strict scrutiny to government actions affecting religion. However, the Supreme Court later ruled the RFRA unconstitutional as it applied to state and local governments, a decision that continues to be controversial today.

The so-called strict scrutiny test required by the RFRA was clearly set forth by the Supreme Court in two cases—*Sherbert v. Verner* (1963) and *Wisconsin v. Yoder* (1972). These cases mandated that courts must find a compelling government interest in order to justify a substantial burden on freedom of religion. Under this test, to be compelling, a government interest must involve relatively important concerns that rise above mere bureaucratic or efficiency goals. Examples of compelling government interests might include national security, protecting citizens' lives, or preserving other constitutional protections. Another part of the strict scrutiny test is that the government must use the least restrictive means to achieve its goal. If the government action that infringes on religious freedom is overbroad, it can still be overturned even if it is a compelling interest.

Later cases weakened the strict scrutiny test in cases involving issues of religion. The main example is the case of *Employment Division v. Smith* (1990), where the Supreme Court ruled that the government could deny unemployment benefits to a person fired for using peyote, an illegal hallucinogenic drug, even though the peyote was used as part of a native American religious ceremony. This and other cases established the principle that the government could restrict religious freedom by passing or enforcing laws of general applicability that apply to all religions without discrimination.

The RFRA, signed into law on November 16, 1993, was a reaction to this looser interpretation of freedom of religion and sought to reinstate the *Sherbert* strict scrutiny test. The question of whether the RFRA was constitutional soon became the subject of a number of lawsuits, and eventually the case of *Boerne v. Flores* reached the Supreme Court. In *Boerne*, the Court was presented with the question of whether a local government's refusal to allow the Roman Catholic Archdiocese of San Antonio to expand a church in Boerne, Texas, violated the RFRA. The Archdiocese argued that the city's denial of a permit to tear down part of the church and expand it to accommodate a growing congregation (because it was located in a historic district) was a substantial burden on freedom of religion without a compelling state interest. The Supreme Court, in a June 1997 decision, ruled that the RFRA was unconstitutional as applied to state and local governments because it exceeded Congress' constitutional enforcement powers. The RFRA, the Court explained, was an attempt by Congress to expand freedom of religion by proscribing government conduct that the constitution does not prohibit. Justice John Paul Stevens clarified the issue when he pointed out that if the church in question happened to be owned by an atheist, there would be no question that the city could deny the permit; thus, the Catholic Church should not get a special exemption from a generally applicable, neutral civil law.

Since the *Boerne* decision, however, a number of states—including Alabama, Arizona, Connecticut, Florida, Idaho, Illinois, New Mexico, Rhode Island, South Carolina, and Texas—have enacted laws patterned after the RFRA. In other states, such as California, Illinois, and Virginia, these types of bills have failed. Critics have challenged these laws as violations of the separation of church and state because they favor religious groups over non-religious groups. Another concern has been that prisoners could use RFRA-type state laws to file frivolous lawsuits claiming that their religious rights are being violated by the restrictions of their imprisonment. At the federal level, the US Congress has also considered but rejected laws that would have replaced the RFRA. The Religious Liberty Protection Act of 2000 (RLPA), for example, passed in the House of Representatives but died in the Senate.

Most notably, although *Boerne* clearly held the RFRA unconstitutional for states and local governments, the law still applies to actions by the federal government. The Supreme Court recently applied the RFRA compelling interest test, for example, in *Gonzales v. O Centro Espirita Beneficente Uniao do Vegetal* (2006), a case that involved the government's seizure of a sacramental tea that contained an illegal drug from a church in New Mexico. The Court found that the government did not have a compelling interest in seizing illegal substances from the church.

Whether the federal RFRA or similar state statutes will herald the birth of expanded protections for freedom of religion in the United States remains to be seen, but it is clear that many religious groups will continue to push for this result. In addition to the RFRA approach, religious advocates are proposing federal- and state-level constitutional amendments to clarify that infringements of religious practices by governments require a compelling state interest. The authors of viewpoints in this chapter discuss these amendments and other issues relevant to how the United States should balance religion and politics in the future.

President Barack Obama Should Support a Constitutional Amendment to Secure Religious Freedom

Rodney K. Smith

Rodney K. Smith is a First Amendment scholar and a professor of law at the Thomas Jefferson School of Law in San Diego, California.

Religious freedom in America is under attack from the right and the left. James Madison, the father of our Constitution, referred to the right of conscience as "the most sacred of all property"—our greatest possession.

That right is increasingly insecure. Under his expansive health care initiative President [Barack] Obama mandated that all institutions provide insurance coverage for contraceptives, including the morning-after pill, even though this mandate violated the religious conscience of Roman Catholics.

The Obama administration narrowly averted a major political crisis when it later agreed to "balance" the government mandate by accommodating the free-exercise rights of Catholics. But now critics say the adjustment doesn't fully exempt the church from funding coverage for birth control, calling it a "shell game." And leaders in the Catholic church have said the compromise amounts to a "hill of beans" and have vowed legal action.

Religious Freedom Under Attack

What is clear is that Mr. Obama had the power—and still does—to disregard the right of conscience, if political winds blew in another direction. Does the president really support the freedom of conscience or is his gesture a politically motivated charade?

Perhaps, but the trend away from religious freedom has been under attack long before the Obama decision.

In 1990, Justice [Antonin] Scalia, a conservative member of the Supreme Court, authored a decision in *Employment Division v. Smith,* a case considering whether the state of Oregon could deny unemployment benefits to two Native American men for their use of peyote (a cactus with psychoactive properties when ingested), whose use and possession is illegal in the state, in the Native American Church.

It isn't hard to predict that government will eventually extend its regulatory tentacles into private faith-based education, health care, and even social services.

With his ruling, Mr. Scalia rejected past Court precedent that provided stronger protection for the right of religious conscience—precedent that had served our nation well. Largely ignoring the track record under the old rule, his opinion stated that to exempt the men from penalties for their religious use of peyote would "make the professed doctrines of religious belief superior to the law of the land, and in effect to permit every citizen to become a law unto himself."

Scalia essentially enunciated a new rule that permits the federal government to violate religious conscience so long as it does so with a general law that is not directly intended to discriminate against religious exercise. In that single act, the Court reduced religious conscience from a right to a mere privilege.

The response to Scalia's opinion was dramatic. Congress, overwhelmingly and with strong support from President [Bill] Clinton, passed the Religious Freedom Restoration Act of 1994, restoring a robust right of conscience. Unfortunately, in

City of Boerne v. Flores, decided in 1997, the Court held that Congress had exceeded it powers, effectively leaving Obama free to disregard religious conscience in his health care initiative.

With the growth of government, religious conscience will likely continue to fall victim to these so-called general laws. It isn't hard to predict that government will eventually extend its regulatory tentacles into private faith-based education, health care, and even social services.

An Old Conflict

This conflict over religious freedom and the reach of government is not new. George Mason and James Madison disagreed over the scope of the right of religious conscience when Virginia was adopting a declaration of rights.

Mason and Madison both acknowledged that religion is a duty owed our Creator. Mason, however, believed that while religious conscience "should enjoy the fullest toleration," government was free to regulate conscience if it "disturb[ed] the peace, the happiness, or safety of society."

[James] Madison understood what [US Supreme Court Justice Antonin] Scalia and [Barack] Obama evidently do not, that conscience is our most significant possession.

Alarmed that Mason had transformed the most sacred of rights into a mere privilege granted by tolerant lawmakers, Madison responded that free exercise could only be limited when the exercise of that right deprived another of an "equal liberty" and when that exercise of conscience "manifestly endangered" the "existence of the state."

For Mason, like Obama and Scalia, religious exercise was a privilege at the mercy of government. Madison, however, saw it as an inalienable right largely beyond the reach of government. Madison's view became the basis for our First Amendment.

Madison understood what Scalia and Obama evidently do not, that conscience is our most significant possession.

Dr. Martin Luther King, Jr., had an experience during the early stages of the civil rights movement that demonstrated the importance of the right of conscience.

One night, Dr. King received a vicious call threatening his family. As he worried about his family, he realized "religion had to become real . . . [he] had to know God for [himself]." He prayed, "Lord, I'm down here trying to do what's right. . . . I think the cause we represent is right. But Lord . . . I'm losing my courage. And I can't let the people see me like this because if they see me weak . . . they will begin to get weak."

King heard an inner voice saying, "Martin Luther, stand up for righteousness. Stand up for justice. Stand up for truth. And lo I will be with you, even until the end of the world." He was "called" to lead a movement that transformed America.

Recognizing the importance of conscience King taught that, "If you haven't found something worth dying for, you aren't fit to be living."

Madison would see Dr. King's religious conscience as a right, not a mere gift from an occasionally tolerant government. It seems that Obama would have us believe that he would recognize it as a right as well, but his actions indicate he may not.

The Need for a Constitutional Amendment

If Obama, Scalia, and others continue their overreach and disregard for this fundamental right of conscience, religious freedom in America will remain insecure. If Obama genuinely supports religious liberty, he can step forward and offer his support for an amendment adopting the language of the Religious Freedom Restoration Act of 1994.

That amendment would restore religious liberty by requiring that the government prove that its regulation of religious exercise is necessary to a compelling state interest. The amendment would also require the government to prove that the regulation is the least restrictive manner in which the government's compelling interest can be achieved.

That amendment would recognize that religious liberty is not a mere privilege. It would restore our most sacred possession—the *right* of religious conscience.

Religious Rights vs. the Public's Right

Oliver Thomas

Oliver Thomas is an author and a member of the board of contributors for USA Today, *a daily national newspaper.*

Religion is a tricky business. It can bring out the best in a person. Think Mahatma Gandhi, Albert Schweitzer or Mother Teresa. But it can also bring out the worst. Think 9/11, the Inquisition or the Salem witch trials. What I'm saying is that religion can short-circuit your ability to think. You sometimes can't see things as they really are because irrational beliefs get in the way. I'll give you a couple of examples.

In New York, ultra-Orthodox Jews are criticizing the Brooklyn district attorney for prosecuting Jewish child sex-abuse cases, according to *The New York Times*. The newspaper reports that a 16-year-old ultra-Orthodox Jewish boy was being molested in a Jewish ritual bathhouse in Brooklyn. After his father reported the crime to police, the father said he was shunned, cursed and kicked out of his apartment by other ultra-Orthodox Jews for trying to protect his son.

In California, inmate Billy Paul Birdwell argued that his religion, Asatru-Odinism, required him to have open space and a fire pit. Prison officials gave him the open space and even built a fence around it. But when officials later replaced that space with a non-denominational outdoor area, Birdwell complained that his religious needs weren't met. Starting to get the picture? To people living within a particular religious tradition, the beliefs always seem reasonable. But there are limits to how far we as a nation can go in protecting the rights of citizens to exercise their faith.

A Step Too Far

Now, North Dakota is getting into the act by pushing for a state constitutional amendment to allow for even more religious freedom. If approved by voters on June 12, the change could result in even more bizarre outcomes over religion.

For decades, the U.S. employed a test for deciding these cases that balanced the religious liberty rights of the individual against the public's right to maintain a civil society. The test went like this. If the government placed a "substantial burden" on a person's religiously motivated behavior, the government must show that the burden was (1) in furtherance of a "compelling" interest, such as health and safety, and (2) was the least burdensome means of accomplishing that interest. The test worked well for years. Religious claimants won some and lost some. Then the Supreme Court changed the rules.

In a case involving the use of peyote by Native Americans, the high court held that it was no longer necessary for government to justify restrictions on religious exercise unless the religion was being singled out for discriminatory treatment.

Of course, legislative bodies generally don't single out particular religions for special burdens. They pass laws that say no one can drink wine in a particular county, and suddenly Catholics have a problem celebrating the Mass. Or they say everyone has to wear a hard hat, and Sikhs—who must wear a turban instead—can no longer get a construction job. Nearly all burdens on religious exercise are caused by laws of general application.

States Take Priority

So you can guess what happened. Religious groups began having problems. Government, to a large measure, stopped accommodating religious exercise. Congress corrected the problem through the "Religious Freedom Restoration Act"—which returned things to the way they were before the peyote ruling. But the Supreme Court would not allow Congress to correct the states. That had to be done by the states themselves. Some 16 legislatures have done precisely that. In other places, the state Supreme Court has stepped in to provide similar protections by interpreting their own constitutions in ways that protect religious exercise.

Either way, America is the better for it. Orthodox Jewish boys can wear their yarmulkes to school, Muslim girls can wear their head scarves, Jewish prisoners can get a kosher meal and evangelical Christians can home-school their children without fear of reprisal from the state.

But some religious Americans want more. Unsatisfied with the First Amendment balancing test, they now want to tilt the playing field. Several states are considering these more radical remedial measures.

North Dakota's proposed constitutional amendment, for example, would eliminate the requirement that a government-imposed burden be "substantial." Any burden would trigger strict scrutiny. The amendment states that even "indirect" burdens, such as withholding benefits, assessing penalties or excluding people from programs would be prohibited. So not only may you home-school your child, you might even be able to force taxpayers to pay for your child to attend a parochial school.

If this is making you nervous, it should. It carries a faint odor of theocracy. Religious freedom may be the crown jewel of our 236-year-old experiment in liberty, but few of us would like to return to Puritan New England. Perhaps it is time for lovers of liberty, including religionists of all stripes, to say "enough."

Religious Institutions Operating Public Accommodations Must Obey Secular Laws

Armando Lloréns-Sar

Armando Lloréns-Sar is a feature writer for the Daily Kos, *a political blog that publishes news and commentary from a progressive viewpoint.*

In 2006, then-Sen. Barack Obama gave a speech on religion in the public square. Obama said:

> Conservative leaders have been all too happy to exploit this gap, consistently reminding evangelical Christians that Democrats disrespect their values and dislike their Church, while suggesting to the rest of the country that religious Americans care only about issues like abortion and gay marriage; school prayer and intelligent design.

> Democrats, for the most part, have taken the bait. At best, we may try to avoid the conversation about religious values altogether, fearful of offending anyone and claiming that—regardless of our personal beliefs—constitutional principles tie our hands.

> At worst, there are some liberals who dismiss religion in the public square as inherently irrational or intolerant, insisting on a caricature of religious Americans that paints them as fanatical, or thinking that the very word "Christian" describes one's political opponents, not people of faith.

I consider it one of Obama's worst speeches ever. On the substance, it is nonsense—accepting of Republican nostrums on "what Democrats think," and then proposing ridiculous ideas for "religion in the public square." As a question of politics, it was a failure as its intent was to inoculate Obama from attack on "lack of faith" grounds from the "Religious Right." Kenyan socialist Muslim anyone? But if that speech was the end of it, well, politics is what it is. But it has not ended there.

[Journalist] E.J. Dionne, joining the most radical elements of the "Religious" Right, has led the "progressive" Catholic attack on the principle of separation of church and state. Dionne points to Obama's 2006 speech as the beacon to follow on this issue, rejecting in essence the famous formulations of JFK's 1960 speech on the issue.

The Encroachment of Religion into Government

The encroachment of religion on our secular government proceeds at an alarming pace.

Last Thursday, the United States Senate narrowly rejected, by a 51-48 vote, passage of the Blunt Amendment, also known as the "Respect for Rights of Conscience Act." The amendment would:

> [Amend] the Patient Protection and Affordable Care Act (PPACA) to permit a health plan to decline coverage of specific items and services that are contrary to the religious beliefs of the sponsor, issuer, or other entity offering the plan or the purchaser or beneficiary (in the case of individual coverage) without penalty. [...] Declares that nothing in PPACA shall be construed to authorize a health plan to require a provider to provide, participate in, or refer for a specific item or service contrary to the provider's religious beliefs or moral convictions. Prohibits a health plan from being considered to have failed to provide timely or other

access to items or services or to fulfill any other requirement under PPACA because it has respected the rights of conscience of such a provider.

Prohibits an American Health Benefit Exchange (a state health insurance exchange) or other official or entity acting in a governmental capacity in the course of implementing PPACA from discriminating against a health plan, plan sponsor, health care provider, or other person because of an unwillingness to provide coverage of, participate in, or refer for, specific items or services.

The separation of church and state . . . insure[s] free exercise of religion and protect[s] the secular government from the encroachment of religion.

To its credit, the Obama administration opposed the Blunt Amendment:

A proposal being considered in the Senate this week would allow employers that have no religious affiliation to exclude coverage of any health service, no matter how important, in the health plan they offer to their workers. This proposal isn't limited to contraception nor is it limited to any preventive service. Any employer could restrict access to any service they say they object to. This is dangerous and wrong.

The Obama administration believes that decisions about medical care should be made by a woman and her doctor, not a woman and her boss. We encourage the Senate to reject this cynical attempt to roll back decades of progress in women's health.

No word on what E.J. Dionne thinks. However, the Obama administration could be accused of betraying the 2006 words of Sen. Obama by "try[ing] to avoid the conversation about religious values altogether, fearful of offending anyone and claiming that—regardless of our personal beliefs—constitutional principles tie our hands." After all, if you provide "accommodations" to religiously affiliated institutions regarding their conduct in the secular world, why not to religious persons as well?

The failure was in not championing the separation of church and state as a principle designed to insure free exercise of religion and protect the secular government from the encroachment of religion. This approach protects religion and the state. It is a principle worth fighting for and being proud of the fight. Instead, the Obama administration is now down the path of a convoluted morass of deciding when, and when not to, accommodate religion in our secular government. The line should be easy to find.

In a recent case, much touted by supporters of the Blunt Amendment, the Supreme Court explained where the line should be drawn. The case is *Hosanna-Tabor Evangelical Lutheran Church and School v. Equal Employment Opportunity Commission et al.* Writing for a unanimous Court, Chief Justice [John] Roberts stated:

> Until today, we have not had occasion to consider whether this freedom of a religious organization to select its ministers is implicated by a suit alleging discrimination in employment. The Courts of Appeals, in contrast, have had extensive experience with this issue. Since the passage of Title VII of the Civil Rights Act of 1964, 42 U. S. C. §2000e et seq., and other employment discrimination laws, the Courts of Appeals have uniformly recognized the existence of a "ministerial exception," grounded in the First Amendment, that precludes application of such legislation to claims concerning the employment relationship between a religious institution and its ministers. We agree that there is such a ministerial exception. The members of a religious group put their faith in the hands of their ministers.
>
> Requiring a church to accept or retain an unwanted minister, or punishing a church for failing to do so, intrudes

upon more than a mere employment decision. Such action interferes with the internal governance of the church, depriving the church of control over the selection of those who will personify its beliefs. By imposing an unwanted minister, the state infringes the Free Exercise Clause, which protects a religious group's right to shape its own faith and mission through its appointments.

When a religion decides that it will own public accommodations, such as hospitals, it must abide by our secular laws and regulations.

Religion in the Secular World

When it comes to the religious institution itself and its function as a ministry, the state has no role and must have no role. Thus a religion can choose to not ordinate women or persons of color as ministers. It can apply discriminatory rules in all aspects of its religious institutions, insisting that women be segregated from men, both in the place of worship or on transportation vehicles operated for purposes of the religious institution. (To be sure, the Court is not particularly consistent in application of this principle.)

However, when the religious institution chooses to engage in the secular world, regulated by our secular government, this protection from government regulation and law ends. Thus, when the Hasidim of Brooklyn choose to use public transportation, they are not permitted to enforce their discriminatory views that women must ride in the back of the bus.

When a religion decides that it will own public accommodations, such as hospitals, it must abide by our secular laws and regulations. This is the crucible of the issue today. Consider this *New York Times* editorial:

A wave of mergers between Roman Catholic and secular hospitals is threatening to deprive women in many areas of the country of ready access to important reproductive services. Catholic hospitals that merge or form partnerships with secular hospitals often try to impose religious restrictions against abortions, contraception and sterilization on the whole system.

Here is the line, easy for all to see. The imposition of religion on a secular public accommodation should not be countenanced. In this case, it involves the Catholic Church imposing religious limitations on health care for women at a public hospital. In the case of the Blunt Amendment, the principle is extended to religious persons, not just institutions.

The Proper Role of Religion in Politics

This does not mean that religions and religious persons must be out of the public arena. To the contrary, religions and religious people should be in the arena, like all of us, fighting for our respective views.

I would expect, and defend the right of, religions and religious persons to work to have their views enshrined in our laws. Thus, for those religions who oppose birth control and women's right to choose, I expect them to fight for the overturn of *Griswold v. Connecticut* and *Roe v. Wade*. For those religions who believe in discrimination based on gender, race or sexual orientation, I expect them to be in the public arena fighting for secular laws that encompass their views on these subjects. And for the positive, for those religions and their adherents who oppose the death penalty, aggressive war, and unbridled capitalism, I expect them to be in the public arena fighting for their views.

My expectations are met every day. No religion and no religious person has been excluded nor do they act as if they have been excluded from the public arena. What some demand however is that even when they lose the argument in the public arena, that they get an exception from following our secular laws. That is unacceptable.

It is a principle that no progressive should even contemplate, much less accept. And yet, too many do. Many Democrats and progressives have, to coin a phrase, "taken the bait." We now see more clearly where that path is leading us. It is an unacceptable path.

The United States Should Promote the Christian Ideals of Religious Freedom and Democracy Around the World

Charles J. Chaput

Charles J. Chaput is the archbishop of Denver, Colorado. From 2003 to 2006, he served as a commissioner with the United States Commission on International Religious Freedom (USCIRF), an independent, bipartisan federal body that monitors violations of religious freedom abroad and makes recommendations to the president, the secretary of state, and the Congress.

In his World Day of Peace message earlier this year [2011], Pope Benedict XVI voiced his concern over the worldwide prevalence of "persecution, discrimination, terrible acts of violence and religious intolerance." In reality, we now face a global crisis in religious liberty. As a Catholic bishop, I have a natural concern that Christian minorities in Africa and Asia bear the brunt of today's religious discrimination and violence. Benedict noted this same fact in his own remarks.

But Christians are not the only victims. Data from the Pew Forum on Religion and Public Life are sobering. Nearly 70 percent of the world's people now live in nations—regrettably, many of them Muslim-majority countries, as well as China and North Korea—where religious freedom is gravely restricted.

Principles that Americans find self-evident—the dignity of the human person, the sanctity of conscience, the separation of political and sacred authority, the distinction between secular and religious law, the idea of a civil society pre-existing and distinct from the state—are not widely shared elsewhere. In fact, as Leszek Kolakowski once said, what seemed self-evident to the American Founders "would appear either patently false or meaningless and superstitious to most of the great men that keep shaping our political imagination." We need to ask ourselves why this is the case.

We cannot understand the framework of American institutions . . . if we don't acknowledge that they grow out of a predominantly Christian worldview.

We also need to ask ourselves why we Americans seem to be so complacent about our own freedoms. In fact, nothing guarantees that America's experiment in religious freedom, as we traditionally know it, will survive here in the United States, let alone serve as a model for other countries in the future. The Constitution is a great achievement in ordered liberty. But it's just another elegant scrap of paper unless people keep it alive with their convictions and lived witness.

Yet in government, media, academia, in the business community and in the wider culture, many of our leaders no longer seem to regard religious faith as a healthy or a positive social factor. We can sense this in the current administration's ambivalence toward the widespread violations of religious liberty across the globe. We can see it in the inadequacy or disinterest of many of our news media in reporting on religious freedom issues. And we can see it especially in the indifference of many ordinary American citizens.

In that light. I have four points that I'd like to share with you today. They're more in the nature of personal thoughts than conclusive arguments. But they emerge from my years as a Commissioner with the U.S. Commission on International Religious Freedom (USCIRF). and I believe they're true and need to be said. The first three deal with the American experience. The last one deals with whether and how the American experience can apply internationally.

A Christian Worldview

Here's my first point: *The American model of religious liberty is rooted in the thought-world and idea-architecture of the Christian humanist tradition.* We cannot understand the framework of American institutions—or the values that these institutions are meant to promote and defend—if we don't acknowledge that they grow out of a predominantly Christian worldview.

Obviously our laws and public institutions also reflect Jewish scripture, Roman republican thought and practice, and the Enlightenment's rationalist traditions. But as Crane Brinton once observed with some irony, even "the Enlightenment [itself] is a child of Christianity—which may explain for our Freudian times why the Enlightenment was so hostile to Christianity."

The American system of checks and balances, which emphasizes personal responsibility and limited government, reflects fundamental biblical truths.

Whatever it becomes in the future, America was *born* Protestant. And foreign observers often seem to understand that better than we do. As many of you know, Dietrich Bonhoeffer, the German Lutheran scholar and pastor murdered by the Third Reich, taught for a time in New York City in the 1930s. He came away struck by the differences between the American and French revolutionary traditions, and the Christian character of American ideals.

"American democracy," Bonhoeffer said, "is not founded upon the emancipated man but, quite on the contrary, upon the kingdom of God and the limitation of all earthly powers by the sovereignty of God."

As Bonhoeffer saw it, the American system of checks and balances, which emphasizes personal responsibility and limited government, reflects fundamental biblical truths about original sin, the appetite for power and human weakness.

Jacques Maritain, the French Catholic scholar who helped draft the U.N.'s charter on human rights, said much the same. He called our Declaration of Independence "an outstanding lay Christian document tinged with the philosophy of the day."

He also said: "The [American] Founding Fathers were neither metaphysicians nor theologians, but their philosophy of life, and their political philosophy, their notion of natural law and human rights, were permeated by concepts worked out by Christian reason and backed up by an unshakeable religious feeling."

That's my point. At the heart of the American model of public life is a Christian vision of man, government and God.

Now, I want to be clear about what I'm saying here—and also what I'm *not* saying.

I'm *not* saying that America is a "Christian nation." Nearly 80 percent of our people self-describe as Christians. And many millions of them actively practice their faith. But we never have been and never will be a Christian confessional state.

I'm *also* not saying that our Protestant heritage is uniformly good. Some of the results clearly *are* good: America's culture of personal opportunity; respect for the individual; a tradition of religious liberty and freedom of speech; and a reverence for the law. Other effects of Reformation theology have been less happy: radical individualism; revivalist politics; a Calvinist hunger for material success as proof of salvation; an ugly nativist and anti-Catholic streak; a tendency toward intellectual shallowness and disinterest in matters of creed; and a nearly religious, and sometimes dangerous, sense of national destiny and redemptive mission.

None of these sins however—and yes, some of our nation's sins have led to very bitter suffering both here and abroad—takes away from the genius of the American model. This model has given us a free, open and non-sectarian society marked by an astonishing variety of cultural and religious expressions. But our system's success does not result from the procedural mechanisms our Founders put in place. Our system works *precisely* because of the moral assumptions that undergird it. And those moral assumptions have a *religious* grounding.

The American Bill of Rights is not a piece of 18th-century rationalist theory: it is far more the product of Christian history.

Human Rights Guaranteed by God

That brings me to my second point: *At the heart of the American model of religious liberty is a Christian vision of the sanctity and destiny of the human person.*

The great Jesuit scholar, Father John Courtney Murray, stressed that: "The American Bill of Rights is not a piece of 18th-century rationalist theory: it is far more the product of Christian history. Behind it one can see, not the philosophy of the Enlightenment, but the older philosophy that had been the matrix of the common law. The 'man' whose rights are guaranteed in the face of law and government is, whether he knows it or not, the Christian man, who had learned to know his own dignity in the school of Christian faith."

I believe that's true. It's a crucial insight. And it's confirmed by other scholarship, including Harold Berman's outstanding work in the history of Western law, and his study of religious liberty and America's founding. My point here is that the institutions and laws in what we call the "Western world" presume a Christian anthropology; a Christian definition of the meaning of life. In the American model, the human person is not a product of nature or evolution. He is not a creature of the state or the economy. Nor, for that matter, is he the slave of an impersonal heaven. Man is first and fundamentally a *religious* being with intrinsic worth, a free will and inalienable rights. He is created *in the image of* God, *by* God and *for* God. Because we are born for God, we belong to God. And any claims that Caesar may make on us, while important, are secondary.

In the vision of America's Founders, God endows each of us with spiritual freedom and inherent rights so that we can fulfill our duties toward him and each other. Our rights come from God, not from the state. Government is justified only insofar as it secures those natural rights, promotes them and defends them.

And this is not just the curious view of some religious shaman. Nearly all the men who drew up our founding documents held this same belief. Note what James Madison said in his "Memorial and Remonstrance against Religious Assessments" in 1785:

"[Man's duty of honoring God] is precedent both in order of time and degree of obligation to the claims of civil society. Before any man can be considered as a member of civil society, he must be considered as a subject of the Governor of the universe."

The American logic of a society based on God's sovereignty . . . has also proven itself remarkably capable of self-criticism, repentance, reform and renewal.

That is why *religious* freedom is humanity's first and most important freedom. Our first governor is God, our Creator, the Governor of the universe. We are created for a religious purpose. We have a religious destiny. Our right to pursue this destiny *precedes* the state. Any attempt to suppress our right to worship, preach, teach, practice, organize and peacefully engage society because of our belief in God is an attack not only on the cornerstone of human dignity, but also on the identity of the American experiment.

I want to add one more thing here: The men who bequeathed us the American system, including the many Christians among them, had a legion of blind spots. Some of those flaws were brutally ugly—slavery, exploitation of the Native peoples, greed, and ethnic and religious bigotry, including a crude anti-Catholicism that remains the most vivid religious prejudice this country has ever indulged.

But the American logic of a society based on God's sovereignty and the sanctity of the human person has also proven itself remarkably capable of self-criticism, repentance, reform and renewal.

Religion Essential to U.S. Democracy

This brings me to my third point: *In the American model, religion is more than a private affair between the individual believer and God. Religion is essential to the virtues needed for a free people. Religious groups are expected to make vital contributions to the nation's social fabric.*

The American experience of personal freedom and civil peace is inconceivable without a religious grounding, and a specifically Christian inspiration.

For all their differences, America's Founders agreed that a free people cannot remain free and self-governing without religious faith and the virtues that it fosters. John Adams' famous words to the Massachusetts militia in 1789 were typical: "Our constitution was made only for a moral and religious people. It is wholly inadequate to the government of any other."

When the Founders talked about religion, they meant something much more demanding and vigorous than the vague "spirituality" in vogue today. Harold Berman showed that the Founders understood religion in a frankly Christian-informed sense. Religion meant "both belief in God and belief in an after-life of reward for virtue, and punishment for sin." In other words, religion *mattered*—personally and socially. It was more than a private preference. It made people *live differently*. People's faith was assumed to have broad implications, including the political kind.

From the beginning, believers—alone and in communities—have shaped American history simply by trying to live their faith in the world. As Nathaniel Hawthorne saw so well, too many of us do it badly, with ignorance and hypocrisy. But enough believers in every generation have done it well enough, long enough, to keep the animating spirit of our country's experiment in ordered liberty alive.

Or to put it another way, the American experience of personal freedom and civil peace is inconceivable without a religious grounding, and a specifically Christian inspiration. What we believe about God shapes what we believe about man. And what we believe about man shapes what we believe about the purpose and proper structure of human society.

The values enshrined in the American model touch the human heart universally.

The differences among Christian, atheist, Hindu, Jewish and Muslim thought are not "insurmountable." *But they are also not "incidental."* Faith, sincerely believed or sincerely refused, has consequences. As a result, theology and anthropology have serious, long term, social and political implications. And papering those differences over with a veneer of secular pieties does *not* ensure civil peace. It ensures conflict—because religious faith touches on the most fundamental elements of human identity and destiny, and its expression demands a public space.

Applying Christian Values to Other Countries

This brings me to my fourth and final point: *I believe that the American model does work and that its principles can and should be adapted by other countries.* But with this caveat. The Christian roots of our ideals have implications. It's impossible to talk honestly about the American model of religious freedom without acknowledging that it is, to a significant degree, the product of Christian-influenced thought. Dropping this model on non-Christian cultures—as our country learned from bitter experience in Iraq—becomes a very dangerous exercise. One of the gravest mistakes of American policy in Iraq was to overestimate the appeal of Washington-style secularity, and to underestimate the power of religious faith in shaping culture and politics.

Nonetheless, I do believe that the values enshrined in the American model touch the human heart universally. We see that in the democracy movements now sweeping the Middle East and North Africa. The desires for freedom and human dignity live in all human beings. These yearnings are not culturally conditioned, or the result of imposed American or Western ideals. They're inherent to all of us.

The modern world's system of international law is founded on this assumption of universal values shared by people of all cultures, ethnicities and religions. The Spanish Dominican priest, Francisco de Vitoria, in the 16th century envisioned something like the United Nations. An international rule of law is possible, he said, because there is a "natural law" inscribed in the heart of every person, a set of values that are universal, objective, and do not change. John Courtney Murray argued in the same way. The natural law tradition presumes that men and women are religious by nature. It presumes that we are born with an innate desire for transcendence and truth.

These assumptions are at the core of the 1948 Universal Declaration of Human Rights. Many of the people who worked on that Declaration, like Jacques Maritain, believed that this charter of international liberty reflected the American experience.

Article 18 of the Declaration famously says that "Everyone has the right to freedom of thought, conscience and religion; this right includes freedom to change his religion or belief; and freedom, either alone or in community with others and in public or private, to manifest his religion or belief in teaching, practice, worship and observance."

A healthy distinction between the sacred and the secular, between religious law and civil law, is foundational to free societies.

In a sense, then, the American model has already been applied. What we see today is a repudiation of that model by atheist regimes and secular ideologies, and also unfortunately by militant versions of some non-Christian religions. The global situation is made worse by the inaction of our own national leadership in promoting to the world one of America's greatest qualities: religious freedom.

This is regrettable because we urgently need an honest discussion on the relationship between Islam and the assumptions of the modern democratic state. In diplomacy and in interreligious dialogue we need to encourage an Islamic public theology that is both faithful to Muslim traditions and also open to liberal norms. Shari'a law [Islamic law] is not absolution. Christians living under shari'a uniformly experience it as offensive, discriminatory and a grave violation of their human dignity.

A healthy distinction between the sacred and the secular, between religious law and civil law, is foundational to free societies. Christians, and especially Catholics, have learned the hard way that the marriage of Church and state rarely works. For one thing, religion usually ends up the loser, an ornament or house chaplain for Caesar. For another, *all theocracies are utopian*—and every utopia ends up persecuting or murdering the dissenters who can't or won't pay allegiance to its claims of universal bliss. . . .

The Pilgrim's Progress . . . [John Bunyan's book about the Puritans, early settlers in North America] is the second most widely read book in the Western world, next only to the Bible. But the same Puritan spirit that created such beauty and genius in Bunyan also led to Oliver Cromwell, the Salem witch trials and the theocratic repression of other Protestants and, of course, Catholics.

Americans have learned from their own past. The genius of the American founding documents is the balance they achieved in creating a civic life that is non-sectarian and open to all: but also dependent for its survival on the mutual respect of secular and sacred authority. The system works. We should take pride in it as one of the historic contributions this country has made to the moral development of people worldwide. We need to insist that religious freedom—a person's right to freely worship, preach, teach and practice what he or she believes, including the right to freely change or end one's religious beliefs under the protection of the law—is a foundation stone of human dignity. No one, whether acting in the name of God or in the name of some political agenda or ideology, has the authority to interfere with that basic human right.

This is the promise of the American model. The Founders of this country, most of them Christian, sought no privileges for their kind. They would not force others to believe what they believed. Heretics would not be punished. They knew that the freedom to believe must include the freedom to change one's beliefs or to stop believing altogether. Our Founders did not lack conviction. Just the opposite. They had enormous confidence in the power of their own reason—but also in the sovereignty of God and God's care for the destiny of every soul.

America was born, in James Madison's words, to be "an asylum to the persecuted and oppressed of every nation and religion." Right now in America, we're not acting like we revere that legacy, or want to share it, or even really understand it.

And I think we may awake one day to see that as a tragedy for ourselves, and too many others to count.

Organizations to Contact

The editors have compiled the following list of organizations concerned with the issues debated in this book. The descriptions are derived from materials provided by the organizations. All have publications or information available for interested readers. The list was compiled on the date of publication of the present volume; the information provided here may change. Be aware that many organizations take several weeks or longer to respond to inquiries, so allow as much time as possible.

Berkley Center for Religion, Peace, & World Affairs
3307 M St., Suite 200, Washington, DC   20007
(202) 687-5119
e-mail: berkleycenter@georgetown.edu
website: http://berkleycenter.georgetown.edu/rfp

The Berkley Center for Religion, Peace, & World Affairs is a project located at Georgetown University in Washington, DC. It is dedicated to the interdisciplinary study of religion, ethics, and public life through research, teaching, and service. The center explores issues such as the global challenges of democracy and human rights; economic and social development; international diplomacy; and interreligious understanding. The center affirms that a deep examination of faith and values is needed and that the open engagement of religious and cultural traditions with one another can promote peace. The center's website provides book recommendations and is a source for other publications, including papers and articles such as "The Role of Civil Society in Peacebuilding, Conflict Resolution, and Democratization," "Law, Religion, and Liberty of Conscience," and "Water and Faith: Rights, Pragmatic Demands, and an Ethical Lens."

Council on Foreign Relations (CFR)
1777 F St. NW, Washington, DC   20006
(202) 509-8400 • fax: (202) 509-8490
website: www.cfr.org

The Council on Foreign Relations (CFR) is an independent, nonpartisan membership organization, think tank, and publisher. It is composed of more than seventy full-time and adjunct fellows who cover the major regions of the world and important foreign policy issues shaping the current international agenda. CFR publishes in various formats, including videos and transcripts of talks with world leaders and policymakers, the bimonthly magazine *Foreign Affairs*, and numerous articles and op-eds. Examples include "Religion and Politics in America" and "Islam and Politics."

The Heritage Foundation
214 Massachusetts Ave. NE, Washington, DC 20002-4999
(202) 546-4400
website: www.heritage.org

The Heritage Foundation is a conservative think tank that researches, formulates, and promotes conservative policies based on the principles of free enterprise, limited government, individual freedom, and a strong national defense. The foundation's targeted audiences include members of Congress, key congressional staff members, policymakers in the executive branch, national news media, and the academic and policy communities. The Heritage Foundation website is a source of many articles, including "Obama v. Religious Liberty: How Legal Challenges to the HHS Contraceptive Mandate Will Vindicate Every American's Right to Freedom of Religion," "Defending Religious Liberty for All," and "Let Religious Freedom Ring: Stop the Assault on Our First Freedom."

Institute on Religion & Democracy (IRD)
1023 Fifteenth St. NW, Suite 601
Washington, DC 20005-2601
(202) 682-4131 • fax: (202) 682-4136
e-mail: info@theird.org
website: www.theird.org

The Institute on Religion & Democracy (IRD) is an ecumenical alliance of American Christians working to reform their churches' social programs in accord with biblical Christian teachings and to contribute to the renewal of a democratic society at home and abroad. IRD is committed to biblical and traditional teachings, to upholding democratic freedoms in the United States, and extending those freedoms to persecuted and oppressed people around the world. IRD publishes *Faith & Freedom*, a bimonthly magazine covering church news, religious liberty, and social witness topics, and *UMAction Briefing*, a quarterly newsletter for United Methodists working for church renewal. Both of these are available on the IRD website, along with a series of papers on public policy issues. Examples include "What Is the Most Important Environmental Task Facing American Christians Today?" and "Is Marriage Worth Defending?"

Pew Forum on Religion & Public Life
1615 L St. NW, Suite 700, Washington, DC   20036
(202) 419-4550
website: http://projects.pewforum.org

The Pew Forum on Religion & Public Life is a project of the Pew Research Center, a nonpartisan fact tank. The project tries to promote a deeper understanding of issues at the intersection of religion and public affairs by conducting surveys, demographic analyses, and other social science research on important aspects of religion and public life in the United States and around the world. The project also provides a neutral venue for discussions of timely issues through roundtables and briefings. The project's website contains links to numerous publications relevant to religion and politics, including: "Little Voter Discomfort with Romney's Mormon Religion," "Catholics Share Bishops' Concerns about Religious Liberty," and "Public Views of the Divide Between Religion and Politics."

Politics of Religious Freedom
e-mail: pennyismay@berkeley.edu
website: http://iiss.berkeley.edu

Politics of Religious Freedom is a three-year project (2011– 2014) designed to examine how religious freedom is being transformed through legal and political processes in the United States, the Middle East, South Asia, and the European Union. Funded by the Henry R. Luce Initiative on Religion and International Affairs, the project is based at the University of California, Berkeley, and at Northwestern University in Evanston, Illinois, and it is also affiliated with Indiana University in Bloomington and University of Maryland Law in Baltimore. The project works with academics, key human rights and civil society organizations, and jurists and policymakers. The project's website is a source of various publications on religion and politics. Examples include "Good Muslim, Bad Muslim," "Believing in Religious Freedom," and "Religious Freedom, Minority Rights, and Geopolitics."

Bibliography

Books

David Brody

The Teavangelicals: The Inside Story of How the Evangelicals and the Tea Party Are Taking Back America. Grand Rapids, MI: Zondervan, 2012.

Walter Brueggemann

The Practice of Prophetic Imagination: Preaching an Emancipatory Word. Minneapolis, MN: Fortress Press, 2012.

E.J. Dionne Jr.

Our Divided Political Heart: The Battle for the American Idea in an Age of Discontent. New York: Bloomsbury USA, 2012.

Colonel V. Doner

Christian Jihad: Neo-Fundamentalists and the Polarization of America. Littleton, CO: Samizdat Creative, 2012.

Robert Booth Fowler et al.

Religion and Politics in America: Faith, Culture, and Strategic Choices. Boulder, CO: Westview Press/Perseus Books Group, 2010.

Jonathan Haidt

The Righteous Mind: Why Good People Are Divided by Politics and Religion. New York: Pantheon Books/Random House, 2012.

Charles Kimball — *When Religion Becomes Lethal: The Explosive Mix of Politics and Religion in Judaism, Christianity, and Islam.* San Francisco, CA: Jossey-Bass/Wiley, 2011.

Stéphane Lacroix — *Awakening Islam: The Politics of Religious Dissent in Contemporary Saudi Arabia.* Cambridge, MA: Harvard University Press, 2011.

Frank Lambert — *Religion in American Politics: A Short History.* Princeton, NJ: Princeton University Press, 2008.

Mark Lilla — *The Stillborn God: Religion, Politics, and the Modern West.* New York: Knopf, 2007.

Andrew C. McCarthy — *The Grand Jihad: How Islam and the Left Sabotage America.* New York: Encounter Books, 2012.

Pippa Norris and Ronald Inglehart — *Sacred and Secular: Religion and Politics Worldwide.* Cambridge, UK: Cambridge University Press, 2004.

Matt Taibbi — *The Great Derangement: A Terrifying True Story of War, Politics, and Religion at the Twilight of the American Empire.* New York: Spiegel & Grau, 2008.

Monica Duffy Toft, Daniel Philpott, and Timothy Samuel Shah — *God's Century: Resurgent Religion and Global Politics.* New York: Norton, 2011.

Kenneth D. Wald and Allison Calhoun-Brown — *Religion and Politics in the United States.* Lanham, MD: Rowman & Littlefield, 2010.

Robert Wuthnow — *Red State Religion: Faith and Politics in America's Heartland.* Princeton, NJ: Princeton University Press, 2012.

Periodicals and Internet Sources

David E. Campbell and Robert D. Putnam — "God and Caesar in America: Why Mixing Religion and Politics Is Bad for Both," *Foreign Affairs,* March/April 2012. www.foreign affairs.com.

Catholic League for Religious and Civil Rights — "Okay to Mix Politics and Religion," June 29, 2012. www.catholic league.org.

CBS News — "Andrew Sullivan: There's So Much Bad Religion Right Now," April 7, 2012. www.cbsnews.com.

Timothy M. Dolan — "ObamaCare and Religious Freedom," *Wall Street Journal,* January 25, 2012.

Richard Allen Greene — "Religious Persecution Is Widespread, Report Warns," CNN, April 29, 2010. http://articles.cnn.com.

Gary Gutting — "The Opinionator: Should Religion Play a Role in Politics?" *New York Times,* July 27, 2011.

Kate Hicks   "Obama vs. Catholics: The War on
                       Religious Freedom," Townhall.com,
                       February 7, 2012. http://townhall
                       .com.

John Hilton   "Will 'Teavangelicals' Turn the
                       Obama/Romney Tide?" Belief and
                       Beyond, July 9, 2012. www.york
                       blog.com/faith.

Elizabeth   "The Tragedy of Religious Freedom
Shakman Hurd   in Syria," *Chicago Tribune News*,
                       March 29, 2012. http://articles
                       .chicagotribune.com.

Charles C.   "Understanding Obama: Why
Johnson   Muslims Get Religious Freedom and
                       Catholics Need Not Apply," *Breitbart*,
                       February 15, 2012. www.breitbart
                       .com.

Jaweed Kaleem   "Religion and Politics Don't Mix,
                       Major Religious Groups Tell
                       Presidential Candidates," *Huffington
                       Post*, February 21, 2012. www
                       .huffingtonpost.com.

Meris Lutz   "Majority of Muslims Want Islam in
                       Politics, Poll Says," *Los Angeles Times*,
                       December 6, 2010. http://articles
                       .latimes.com.

Barry Lynn   "On Faith: The Role Religion Should
                       Play in Republican Politics,"
                       Washington Post, August 19, 2011.
                       www.washingtonpost.com.

Eric Marrapodi	"5 Reasons 'Teavangelicals' Matter," CNN Belief Blog, June 27, 2012. http://religion.blogs.cnn.com.
Jonathan Merritt	"The Religious Right Turns 33: What Have We Learned?" *The Atlantic*, June 8, 2012. www.theatlantic.com.
John J. Myers	"The Opinion Pages: Religious Freedom: An American Bishop's View," *New York Times*, May 25, 2012. www.nytimes.com.
Nicole Neroulias	"American Politics More Religious than American Voters," *Huffington Post*, August 22, 2012. www.huffingtonpost.com.
New York Times	"The Politics of Religion," May 27, 2012. www.nytimes.com.
Barack Obama	"Politicians Need Not Abandon Religion," *USA Today*, July 9, 2006. www.usatoday.com.
PBS Newshour	"Romney and 'Teavangelicals': Gaining Trust with Conservative Voters," July 10, 2012. www.pbs.org/newshour.
Kirsten Powers	"America's Naivete About Egypt," *The Daily Beast*, February 3, 2011. www.thedailybeast.com.
Reince Priebus	"Obama's Assault on Religious Freedom," *Politico*, February 8, 2012. http://dyn.politico.com.

Winnifred Fallers Sullivan — "We Are All Religious Now. Again," *Social Research*, Vol. 76, No. 4, Winter 2009.

Winnifred Fallers Sullivan, Elizabeth Shakman Hurd, and Peter Danchin — "The Global Securitization of Religion," Social Science Research Council, March 23, 2010. http://blogs.ssrc.org.

Loretta Sword — "Should Religion Play a Role in Politics?" *Pueblo Chieftain*, February 11, 2012. www.chieftain.com.

Scott M. Thomas — "A Globalized God: Religion's Growing Influence in International Politics," *Foreign Affairs*, November/December 2010. www.foreignaffairs.com.

Index

A

B

C